CROW PLANET

ALSO BY Lyanda Lynn Haupt

Pilgrim on the Great Bird Continent
Rare Encounters with Ordinary Birds

CROW PLANET

Essential Wisdom from the
Urban Wilderness

Lyanda Lynn Haupt

Little, Brown and Company

New York   Boston   London

Little, Brown and Company
Hachette Book Group
237 Park Avenue, New York, NY 10017
Visit our Web site at www.HachetteBookGroup.com

First Edition: July 2009

Little, Brown and Company is a division of Hachette Book Group, Inc. The Little, Brown name and logo are trademarks of Hachette Book Group, Inc.

The excerpt from "Crows" is from *New and Selected Poems* by Mary Oliver, copyright © 1992 by Mary Oliver. Reprinted by permission of Beacon Press, Boston.

Illustrations by Daniel Cautrell

Library of Congress Cataloging-in-Publication Data

Haupt, Lyanda Lynn.
Crow planet : essential wisdom from the urban wilderness / Lyanda Lynn Haupt. — 1st ed.
        p. cm.
    Includes bibliographical references and index.
    ISBN-13: 978-0-316-01910-1
    1. Crows—Anecdotes.   I. Title.
    QL696.P2367H37 2009
    598.8'64—dc22   2008028555

10 9 8 7 6 5 4 3 2 1

RRD-IN

Printed in the United States of America

For my radiant daughter, Claire

—a friend to slugs, spiders,
birds, and the wild earth

Crows

From a single grain they have multiplied.
When you look in the eyes of one
you have seen them all.

At the edges of highways
they pick at limp things.
They are anything but refined.

Or they fly out over the corn
like pellets of black fire,
like overlords.

Crow is crow, you say.
What else is there to say?
Drive down any road,

take a train or an airplane
across the world, leave
your old life behind,

die and be born again —
wherever you arrive
they'll be there first,

glossy and rowdy
and indistinguishable.
The deep muscle of the world.

— MARY OLIVER

CONTENTS

CONTENTS

CROW PLANET

CROWS AND *KAIROS*

An Invocation

By all rights, I should never see the crow who perches almost daily on the electrical wire just beyond my study window. Her story will be told in these pages, and it will become clear, first, that she should be dead and, further, that since she did not die after all, my wire should be the last place that she chooses to land. This young crow is immediately recognizable by her habit of roosting with her belly on the wire rather than perching properly upright, a habit shared by broken-legged crows, who cannot support their full weight or stand on a wire, balancing on just one good foot. I call her Charlotte. (Naming wild animals is problematic, inviting confusion between our relationships with wild and domestic animals, which must be qualitatively different. Still, familiarity breeds naming, and I have been watching this crow every day for months, learning her individual needs, quirks, and habits. Without even thinking about it, I began calling her Charlotte, after the brilliant, self-effacing, fragile-but-brave Charlotte Brontë.)

When Charlotte was an injured fledgling, I gently kidnapped her and held her captive in my bathtub for an entire day, force-feeding her cat food and egg, and splinting her bent leg. Having worked as a wild bird rehabilitator, I possess an instinctual, if not always sensible, impulse to tend to injured birds. Her parent crows—who have continued to tend to the fragile Charlotte long after other adult birds have given off caring for their young of the year, and who often perch on my wire along with her—should, given my offense, take her somewhere else. They all recognize me, of that I am sure. A recent study by John Marzluff, corvid researcher at the University of Washington, confirms that crows can recognize individual human faces. Marzluff noticed that crows he had captured and banded would react negatively to his presence, cawing and dive-bombing whenever he approached. His students, who had also banded crows, experienced the same discrimination from crows in the campus study area. To test the idea that crows were recognizing faces in such instances, rather than clothes, gait, or some other identifying characteristic, Marzluff employed masks. A "dangerous" caveman mask was donned by students who trapped and banded seven campus crows. In the following months, volunteers wearing the caveman mask walked prescribed routes known to be frequented by these crows and their associates. The birds went wild, reading the crow riot act whenever the mask wearers passed. For control purposes, the same volunteers walked their routes wearing a Dick Cheney mask, which had not been worn by the trapper/banders, and the crows left them entirely alone. It appears that crows also learn to dislike individual humans through social learning—if birds in a given group appear to loathe a particular person, other crows in the group will take up this aversion for themselves, uttering a vocal rebuke when the person is spotted or avoiding him entirely.

Many people don't need a study to tell them that crows can pick them out of a crowd. Anyone who has chased a crow, come too close to a crow's active nest, or tried to approach a crow's chick knows that the crows involved, and others watching, will harbor an unforgiving resentment toward the guilty party. For months, and sometimes for years, the perpetrator will be swooped and scolded on sight.

The people whom crows recognize most readily seem to be the ones who come overly near to their young, so actually picking a crow fledgling up and toting it home in broad daylight should be a radically punishable offense in the crow-human societal borderlands. But for some reason, the adult crows who dive-bombed me when I kidnapped Charlotte and again when I returned her to their care never bothered me again. Instead, they cared incessantly for the broken-legged fledgling. They kept her from harm, even though she was weak and broken and by all guesses a hopeless case; they hid her from cats, rats, and raccoons, and they continue to preen and coddle her. While I would expect them to avoid me, they bring Charlotte back to the scene of my crime almost every day and let me see how she's doing. I cannot help thinking that some communication has taken place, that it is somehow clear to the crows that my grievous offense was accomplished in good faith. We all experience such times—don't we?—when our guarded separateness breaks down.

Such a question is timelier now than it has ever been. We live on a changing earth where ecological degradation and global climate change threaten the most foundational biological processes. If the evolution of wild life is to continue in a meaningful way, humans must attain a changed habit of being, one that allows us to recognize and act upon a sense of ourselves as integral to the wider earth community. Fortunately, this will not normally involve the kidnapping of young crows, but it will mean some radical thinking and even more radical doing. In spite of the string of magazine covers announcing the contrary, we all know that ten simple things will not save the earth. There are, rather, three thousand impossible things that all of us must do, and changing our light bulbs, while necessary, is the barest beginning. We are being called upon to act against a prevailing culture, to undermine our own entrenched tendency to accumulate and to consume, and to refuse to define our individuality by our presumed ability to do whatever we want.

It is easy to become cynical about the fact that we as a species appear to have waited until the last possible moment—the moment in which we must radically change our way of living in order to forestall an unprecedented human-caused ecological collapse—and even that, for many, seems not quite enough incentive. It is *easy* to become cynical, but it is not helpful. My ongoing education in the close-to-home wild has reinforced my sense that we are living in an absolutely graced moment, a rare earthly time in which our present, everyday actions are meaningfully entwined with a broader destiny. There are two Greek words for time. One is *chronos,* which refers to the usual, quantifiable sequential version of time by which we monitor and measure our days. The other word is *kairos,* which denotes an unusual period in human history when eternal time breaks in upon chronological time. *Kairos* is "the appointed time," an opportune moment, even a time of crisis, that creates an opportunity for, and in fact demands, a human response. It is a time brimming with meaning, a time more potent than "normal" time. We live in such a time now, when our collective actions over the next several years will decide whether earthly life will continue its descent into ecological ruin and death or flourish in beauty and diversity.

We all know dour environmentalists (or perhaps we are one), wringing their hands while myopically bemoaning the disasters to befall the earth in the near future. Why, when we know that they are right, do we want to spill organic cranberry juice all over their hemp sandals? Because they are *no fun,* for one thing. And, more important, because they will suck us dry if we let them. But we don't have to let them. There is a way to face the current ecological crisis with our eyes open, with stringent scientific knowledge, with honest sorrow over the state of life on earth, with spiritual insight, and with practical commitment. Finding such a way is more essential now than it has ever been in the history of the human species. But such work does not have to be dour (no matter how difficult) or accomplished only out of moral imperative (however real the obligation) or fear (though the reasons to fear are well founded). Our actions can rise instead from a sense of rootedness, connectedness, creativity, and delight. But how are we to attain such intimacy, living at a remove from "nature," as most of us do, in our urban and suburban homes?

In the environmental classic *A Sand County Almanac,* Aldo Leopold proffered a touchstone by which to judge human activity, one that most first-year ecology students have memorized: "A thing is right when it tends to preserve the integrity, stability, and beauty of the biotic community. It is wrong when it tends otherwise." Eco-philosophy has come a long way in the sixty years since Leopold, but no one has managed to improve on his simple measure. In his use of the gentle, open-ended word *tends,* Leopold recognizes that such things are not cut and dried. But he does realize that we cannot judge the leanings of our actions, whether they tend toward preservation or otherwise, from a vantage of pure abstraction, from an urban existence cut off entirely from the cycles of nature. The reckoning Leopold asks of us requires the cultivation of insight based in attention, knowledge, and intimacy. It asks that we pay loving attention to the places we live, to understand their intricate net of connections with the wider earth.

Many nature writers send dispatches from their wooded homes with the brook babbling outside the ever-open window; they go on weeks- or months-long solitary rambles in remote places. They bring us along, in their writing, on these adventures and in the musings they inspire. And they *do* inspire. Certainly, I believe that wilderness experiences are both restorative and essential on many levels. I am constantly contriving to get myself and my family out of the city to go hiking or camping in forests, mountains, and meadows in our Pacific Northwest home and beyond. But in making such experiences the core of our "connection to nature," we set up a chasm between our daily lives ("non-nature") and wilder places ("true nature"), even though it is in our everyday lives, in our everyday homes, that we eat, consume energy, run the faucet, compost, flush, learn, and *live*. It is here, *in our lives,* that we must come to know our essential connection to the wilder earth, because it is here, in the activity of our daily lives, that we most surely affect this earth, for good or for ill.

Clearly, our cities, suburbs, and houses cry out for improvements that reflect ecological knowledge. I am not claiming they are as natural as those places we traditionally think of as Nature or Wilderness. They are not enough. They are, nevertheless, inhabited by spiders, snails, raccoons, hawks, coyotes, earthworms, fungi, snakes, and crows. They are surrounded as surely as any wilderness by clouds, sky, and stars. They are sparsely populated by beautiful, unsung, eccentric-seeming people who have spent decades studying the secret lives of warblers or dragonflies or nocturnal moths or mushrooms. They are our homes, our habitats, our ecosystems.

The title *Crow Planet* has two intertwined meanings. First, it refers to an earth upon which native biodiversity is gravely threatened, where in too many places the rich variety of species is being noticeably replaced by a few prominent, dominant, successful species (such as crows). At the same time, *Crow Planet* alludes to the fact that no matter where we dwell, or how, our lives are implicated in, and informed by, all of wilder life through the insistent presence of native wild creatures (such as crows).

There are more crows now than there have ever been in the history of the earth. There are more people, too, and in fact, the crow-human ratio has remained fairly constant for the last several thousand years. But what has changed, for both species, is density and proximity. The spread of human-made habitations, urban and suburban, has pressed humans and crows into unprecedented nearness, and into an uneasy relationship. Unlike most wild creatures, crows tolerate human habitations and relish the benefits of living within them—mainly the easy food sources. But to say that crows enjoy human company, or even prefer to live near humans, would be an overstatement. Though they may appear bold, most crows live in a constant state of wary readiness. And people, in turn, are vaguely unsettled by crows. Some love crows, some hate them, but nearly everyone respects their intelligence, and nearly everyone has a "crow story" to tell.

The spread of crow-ness is distressing on many levels. Abundant crows are an emblem of rampant habitat destruction and of the creation of an earth that is inhospitable to all but a handful of the most resilient beings. But they also offer an oblique suggestion of hope. The conspicuous presence of a native wild animal, one that struts our sidewalks, simultaneously accepts and balks at our presence, shares our food, and drops its children at our feet for close observation, can lend a great deal to our biological education. Crows can show us how certain wild, nonhuman animals live — what they need, how they speak, how they walk, and how they tip their heads in that special sideways manner to sip the slenderest bit of rainwater. They make us notice just how many of them there are getting to be, to realize that as humans generate the conditions that allow crow populations to grow, many other wild animal species, birds in particular, are present in far fewer numbers and others are gone completely. Crows are wild beings in our midst, even as they point to the wildness that we cannot see and have lost. Their abundance holds a warning but also a promise: no matter how urban or suburban, how worldly-wise and wilderness-blind, no matter how drastically removed we as a culture and as individuals may have become from any sense of wilderness or wildness or the splendid exuberance of nature, we will nevertheless be thrust, however unwittingly, into the presence of a native wild creature on a near-daily basis. This means that, if we are willing to tolerate our crow-related uneasiness and accept certain lessons, there is hope. Hope that we can renew our sense of natural connectedness and integrity. Hope that we can learn another kind of attention that is deeper, wilder, more creative, more native, more difficult, and far more beautiful than that which has come to be accepted as adequate. There is, at least, reason to dwell in hopeful possibility, to believe that humans just might be capable of the momentous, humble, graced actions that will allow the evolution of wild life to continue.*

How, exactly, are we connected to the earth, the more-than-human world, in our lives and in our actions? And in light of this connection, how are we to carry out our lives on a changing earth? These are the questions we are called to answer in this *kairos,* this graced moment of opportune crisis. I have come to believe that opening ourselves to such inquiry and participating daily in the process of discovery it implies is our most urgent work as humans in the new millennium. And not because engaging these questions will make us happier, or smarter, or make more of our moments feel enchanted, though it will certainly do all of these things. It is urgent because an intimate awareness of the continuity between our lives and the rest of life is the only thing that will truly conserve the earth—this wonderful earth that we

---

* Before the 1930s, land managers typically grouped wild animals in one of two ways: *game* was hunted for sport or food, and *wild life* (two words) was a broader category that included the nongame species. It wasn't until the midthirties that all wild animals began to be referred to by the single word *wildlife* in management circles, a move that reflected a deepening public attention to conservation issues rather than just the preservation of game populations for hunting. Unless I am referring only to animals, I like to expansively employ the older term *wild life,* and use it to refer to the whole, complex, life-giving spectrum of earthly existence, whether normally considered to be alive or not—the human and nonhuman, the biological, geological, botanical, and atmospheric.

rightly love. We cannot know a place well or understand to which side of Leopold's *tendency* our actions swing unless we walk the paths and know the breadth of our neighborhood and neighbors, on and off the concrete, above and below the soil.

We can all find our place in this unfolding story. In seeking my own, I have been to the library, the monastery, the backyard, the city parks, the ocean, the wilderness, and the edge of my sanity. I have relinquished, over and over, my attachment to definitive universal answers. Time after time I find that I am misguided, mistaken, lazy, or lost. But I return anyway, to the questions and to the crows. Here, after all, is a bird very much like us — at home, yet not entirely at home in the urban habitat, gleaning what's here while remaining wild, showing us what's beautiful, what's ugly, and what's missing. Crows remind us that we make our homes not in a vacuum, but in a zoöpolis, a place where human and wild geographies meet and mingle. They press us to our own wilder edges. They may step along our sidewalks, but in the next moment they fly off the path. If we want to watch them well, we will have to leave our own accustomed paths, the cultivated places, the neat edges of our yards and minds. We will find that our lives are not as impoverished as we've been told they are; the sidewalk is not as straight as we thought.

A Note on Names and Pronouns

Avian. Scientifically, linguistically, and according to the *Chicago Manual of Style, it* is the third person singular pronoun of choice for crows, and any bird, for that matter. But after hundreds of hours spent watching crows in the past two years, I have seen enough of them as individuals, as members of family groups or winter flocks, and as plain old animals like myself trying to get through the day, to call any crow "it."

On the surface it is almost impossible to tell a male crow from a female. Their plumages are exactly alike. Male crows are on average somewhat larger than females, but any experienced birder will tell you that size is terribly difficult to gauge in the field. Plus, large female crows are sometimes bigger than small male crows, making size a factor but not a definitive indicator of sex. With practice, an observer may learn to tell male from female crows based on behavioral cues with some reliability, particularly during the breeding and nesting season, when we can see males climbing onto the backs of females, and then observe the sexes taking on different roles at the nest. Male crows have more testosterone than females, and this sometimes comes across in their social interactions. But such distinctions can be subtle, and gender calls based on social interactions are risky. When I have a good reason to guess that a crow is either male or female, I refer to it, naturally, as either he or she. When I am unable to reliably determine a crow's sex, I often make an intuitive guess, knowing that I have a 50 percent chance of being wrong (or maybe, so as to give *some* credit to educated intuition, a 45 percent chance), and so, even though I call many crows in this book *he* or *she*, they may actually be the other. I've noticed that whenever I refer to a crow as a she in conversation, I am invariably asked, "How do you know it's a female?" However, if I refer to a bird as a he, no one ever asks how I know it's a male—not ever. Our efforts to move toward inclusive language in our lives and literature seem to have stopped cold in our discussions of the natural history world, where all animals are still neutrally male unless we know better.

Human. When I refer to friends in this book, sometimes I use their real names and sometimes I give them assumed names, depending on their preference. "Dr. Steffan" is a composite character made up of both a real-life therapist and a real-life psychiatrist. His name is invented.

One

GETTING UP

A Reluctant Crow Watcher

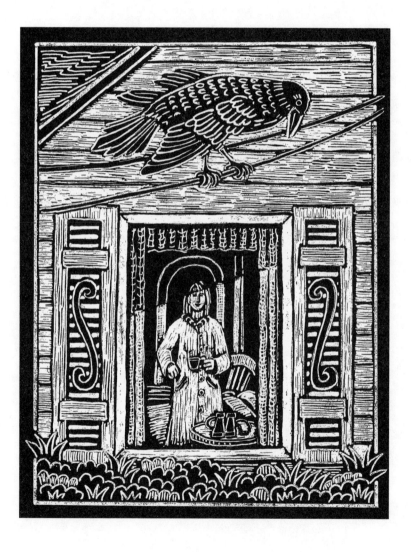

[The crow's caw] mingled with the slight murmur of the village, the sound of children at play, as one stream empties gently into another, and the wild and tame are one. What a delicious sound! It is not merely crow calling to crow, for it speaks to me too. I am part of one great creature with him; if he has voice, I have ears.

— Henry David Thoreau

Crows are not my favorite bird. I never meant to watch crows especially, or to write about them. I am not one of those people who particularly identifies with crows, or has dreamed of them since birth, or believes that crows are my special totem. I've paid perhaps more attention than is usual to crows because they are birds, and I am a life-long student of things ornithological. But I really started to study them only because the editor of my first book told me to. The book was a collection of essays that considers the human relationship with the natural world via birds. I wrote the essays because I was interested in a particular question having to do with a certain species, because something in my studies of these species sparked ideas I felt compelled to write about. But that hadn't happened to me with crows. I knew they were smart and interesting, and I had my own crow stories to tell, as all nominal watchers of birds do, but that was it. Besides, I had already written about starlings in that book, and that seemed to me enough of ultracommon, shiny-black, very urban birds. So when my editor said he'd like to see a crow chapter, I said, well no, I didn't think so. But he insisted, charmingly. And because I was rather in awe of him, and not at all because I wanted to write about crows, I said, reluctantly, okay.

Since I thought I had nothing to say about crows, and since I was in a hurry, I started watching crows constantly, and with some urgency. Just as instructively, I began asking people—normal people, not "bird people"—what they thought about crows. And I've rarely been so surprised. Whenever I ask someone about chickadees or robins or flickers or other common birds that people see with some regularity, the response is almost always lackluster, noncommittal, or at best blandly cheerful. But not so with crows. People's opinions about crows are disproportionately strong. Some *love* crows. *Oh! They are so intelligent! And beautiful!* Others *hate* them. *Loud. Poopy. Evil. A pestilence upon the city.* Another common response, one that I didn't foresee, was a nuanced dis-ease, a shadowy sort of crow ambivalence that runs unusually deep. There is caution over the words chosen: *I know they are smart....I can't say I like them. I don't wish them harm or anything. I'm actually a little afraid of them.* Several women I have spoken with will not walk in parks with their small children if there are too many crows. They cannot tell me why exactly. And surrounding the myriad responses, even among the crow haters, there is nearly always an air of respect—a feeling that crows are, behind their shiny dark eyes, *knowing things.* It is a respect that few songbirds command.

Crows are members of the family Corvidae, which includes not only the various crow species of the world but also all of the jays, magpies, and ravens. Corvids, in turn, belong to the large avian order the Passeriformes, colloquially called the passerines, and even more colloquially the songbirds, which include the thrushes, finches, warblers, sparrows, chickadees, and many others. Passerines have feet built for perching, with three toes pointing forward and one toe pointing back, and sharp, curved toenails. They have nine or ten primary wing feathers, and are often good fliers and gifted songsters. Most passerines have a song particular to the breeding season, which males sing in order to establish a nesting territory and to attract a mate (corvids are exceptions within the order; though known for their vocal facility, they don't have a seasonal "song"). Several species of birds with overall blackish plumage are often confused with the corvids, including blackbirds, grackles, cowbirds, and starlings. All of these are passerines but otherwise not closely related to crows.

Within North America, the Common Raven, *Corvus corax*, is by far the largest bird in the passerine order, followed by the American Crow, *Corvus brachyrhynchos*. In the field guide, and in the field, for that matter, ravens and crows both look like big black birds, and it is not uncommon to think of crows as being pretty much like ravens, just smaller. But there are many differences between the two species, and if we can train ourselves to move beyond our overreliance on color in the identification of birds (as with most other things), it becomes clear that not all the differences are subtle ones.

Ravens *are* indeed larger than crows. An average crow weighs a shy pound and measures sixteen to eighteen inches from tip to tail; a raven weighs 2.5 pounds and is twenty-four inches long. A typical raven's wingspan measures fifty-three inches, while a crow's is usually about thirty-nine inches. Still, it is remarkably difficult, even for experienced observers, to judge size in the field, and unless a crow and a raven are side by side in a tree or in flight, eyeballing the size of the bird is not a reliable factor in determining whether it is a crow or a raven. A raven, though, is shaped differently from a crow. It is bulkier for its size, and its bill is proportionately much larger in relation to its head. Its rictal bristles—the whiskerlike coverings over their nostrils (actually a modified feather)—are usually observable through binoculars at a reasonable range. In flight, the raven's wedge-shaped tail, in contrast to the crow's mainly straight, slightly rounded tail, is a good identifier.

Other attributes of flying crows and ravens are less clear-cut and require a little experience to use reliably, but nearly anyone can manage them eventually. Crows rarely fly very far without flapping their wings, while ravens soar frequently. Crows flap fairly rapidly, and they look as if they are pushing their wings slightly backward, sort of like they are swimming through the air, while ravens have a steadier up-and-down wing beat. Crows are sleek, agile birds in flight, while ravens—though nimble for their size—give an impression of bulkiness. And of course, the raven's low, toadish croak distinguishes it handily from the crow, with its higher, raspier, ultrafamiliar *Caw! Caw!*

The social conventions and habitat requirements of crows and ravens distinguish them further. Ravens are the only bird on earth that can be found just about anywhere on the planet. They inhabit deserts, coastlines, and high mountains. Other geographically ubiquitous birds, such as Red-tailed Hawks, Great Horned Owls, and various species of crow, can be found in all of these regions as well but stop well short of arctic tundra. Amazingly, the Common Raven—the same species found in the Sahara—readily inhabits the frigid arctic reaches. While ravens in some places do gather in feeding congregations, particularly in the winter, they are on the whole far less social and gregarious than crows. And though some ravens turn up in places where humans gather, they are not persistent followers of human habitations like crows are. Crows have come to be closely associated with human dwellings, and some crows, such as the Asian House Crow, are found *only* in places that are populated by humans. (In parts of Japan, the crow population has grown so far out of control that jumpsuit-wearing "crow patrols" are dispatched to destroy nests that, formed atop utility poles, cause electrical blackouts.)

The minds of crows and ravens are also different. Though both species demonstrate remarkable intelligence, ravens generally appear to be able to problem-solve more quickly and at a higher level than crows, working one or two more steps into a multistep problem. Both crows and ravens play—another sign of rich intelligence—but raven games tend to be more complex and may involve a level of "rules" that crow games don't. Where crows will drop a stick in midair and swoop down to catch it, for example, ravens might pair up and take turns dropping the stick for each other. The differences do not necessarily suggest that ravens are more advanced in all areas. Because crows live so gregariously, they may have more developed social norms than ravens — an organized respect for the dead, perhaps, and possibly even a basic system of crow justice. Though such notions are largely anecdotal, there is reason to suppose we will come to understand these dimensions better as our crow watching becomes more sophisticated. Globally there are many species of crow. Unless otherwise noted, my observations in this book pertain to the most ubiquitous North American species, the American Crow.

For the majority of people on the face of the earth, the crow will be the single most oft-encountered native wild animal in their lives. I have never read any study saying that this is so; surely it is an unproven, and probably even an unprovable, claim. But it is likely to be true. Humans gather in villages, suburbs, and urban landscapes, and crows follow them there. The denser and more removed from wild places our dwellings become, the less likely we are to see any wild animals at all other than crows.

Certainly we live alongside other birds, but the most prevalent urban birds besides crows — pigeons, European Starlings, and House Sparrows — are all native to Europe rather than to North America. City green spaces and backyards host a variety of native birds—robins, chickadees, flickers, hummingbirds, and the like. These are a delight to observe, but in most places their numbers do not compare with those of the crows, and the crows, being larger and more vocal, are easier to find and watch. Because of their terrific intelligence, crows also do fabulous things compared with other birds (and even some people), things that catch our notice. Those of us who may be too blinded by our own lack of contact with wild creatures to notice a hummingbird still stumble over crows with habitual regularity.

There are other, nonavian wild animals in the places that humans gather—raccoons, for example. But raccoons are comparatively seldom seen, being mainly nocturnal and far less numerous than crows. Rats are nocturnal as well and desperately secretive. And the majority of urban and suburban rats are not native to the places they now live. Most of the squirrels we see also originated elsewhere. In Seattle, where I live, the parks and gardens are populated by nonnative Eastern gray squirrels, and in any case, there are far more crows than squirrels. After all, squirrels won't stray far from trees; crows are fine with parking lots.

Insects and spiders are certainly more abundant as a group than crows, but, with a few exceptions, such as the large and shockingly beautiful tiger swallowtail butterfly, they are too small and dull colored to be within our sphere of notice. Even when we do notice insects and spiders, such as when they are biting us—and this they prefer to do while we're sleeping—we rarely know how to identify them with any degree of accuracy before we squish them.

So I'm quite confident that this claim—that crows are the most common native wild being that humans regularly see—is true. I've conducted this thought-experiment with an array of biological scientists, and no one can think of a wild animal that is likely to be more familiar, or more regularly encountered, than the crow. And the more we spread our insistent pavement, the more crows we make. As roads and housing developments cut into farmland and forest edges, North America is transformed into a fair crow Eden, and the birds are more urban today than they have ever been. In many places, crow populations are rising exponentially, mirroring, with uncanny exactness, human population growth. While there will be exceptions in certain places and for certain groups of people, most of us must look to the crow as our single most accessible link to native wild things.

"So you're saying crows are the bird we deserve," friends have suggested, as if crows—bulky and black, stalking about—might be present as a punitive reminder of our ecological missteps. It might sound as if that's what I'm saying. Certainly it is ironic, at best, that we remove forests, replace them with concrete and shrubbery, line the sidewalks with plastic cans full of food scraps and topped with ill-fitting lids and then lament the presence and noise of so many crows. But no, if it were about *deserving,* we would have no bird at all. As it is, we have a shiny, black, intelligent, native, wild bird. Crows may not be the bird we deserve, but they are the bird we've been given.

It is difficult to know just how many crows there are.

The international avian conservation organization Partners in Flight estimates the American Crow population in the United States to be about thirty-one million, but some crow experts, including John Marzluff at the University of Washington, believe that number to be a bit low. There are more than three hundred million people in the United States. Marzluff tells me that while he doesn't know for certain, he thinks there might be about one crow for every five to ten humans. This would be consistent with his studies showing that nesting pairs in suburban areas tend to claim and defend two houses with their accompanying yards as breeding territory. There is, then, roughly one crow per family. I like to think about this when I set the table for dinner; I imagine a dark visitor, our allotted crow, perching on the back of a chair with one of our best china plates in front of it, waiting for the spaghetti.

Once crows had insinuated themselves into my thinking, I found it difficult to shake them. How about a book on crows? my editor queried. Absolutely not, I said, fully believing the chapter I'd written had been enough crows for me. But the crows had by now inveigled their way into my brain. I started to find myself and my spotting scope at Alki Beach, a stretch of Puget Sound shoreline near my home, where I could study the crows who pick marine invertebrates from the rocky shore as their main sustenance as they have for thousands of years, from the time when the condos and the Starbucks across from the beach were ancient spruce, fir, and red cedar forests. Besides the Alki group, I began to exhaustively study the crows that frequent my front and backyards. I now study crows wherever I am, but it is to these two groups that I return over and over, and through all the seasons. In the last couple of years, I have logged hundreds of hours, studying the ways of crows. Like Socrates, the more I know, the more I know I don't know. I could not in a lifetime exhaust the subject of crow natural history.

I never intended to live in a city. I was a post-hippie Earth-firster, tree-sitting, ecofeminist, radical birdwatcher, Earth Mother to be. Though I always knew on some level that my utopian vision for my eventual adult life was rather naive, I couldn't help imagining that I would give birth to a girl, and that my daughter would chase butterflies around the acres of meadows and woodlands that surrounded our funky cabinesque home while I murmured sweet nothings into the velvety golden ears of our Jersey cow and led her about by a rope, barefoot, listening to her bell tinkle.

Unsurprisingly, that's not what happened. I rented a little apartment in Seattle where I finished up my master's thesis on environmental ethics and took a job with Seattle Audubon. I met and eventually married my wonderful husband, Tom. I got pregnant, birthed the presaged girl, and decided that I would do what the other primates do—raise my daughter myself rather than hiring strangers to do so.

I resigned from Audubon and wrote my first book during her naps, and my husband commuted by bus from our tiny cottage of a house in West Seattle to his office across the bridge. This was not rural living by any stretch, but it was meaningful and happy. To stave off any latent cow yearnings, I installed a small flock of beautiful backyard chickens.

Eventually we realized that we could manage to buy a bigger house, and we fell in love with a restored 1920s farmhouse with high ceilings, rich fir moldings, a big yard, and koi swimming blithely in a vintage pond that called to mind an ancient Italian grotto. It was just two blocks from a busy road, and not at all in the neighborhood we had envisioned, but despite our reservations, we bought it. I supposed that once we moved there, the pleasure of living in such a pretty house would dispel my lingering doubts. I would put up curtains, plant a new vegetable garden, and be happy. But instead, I fell into a kind of anxious depression, one I attributed (whether oversimplistically or not, I still do not know) to living in the city against the pull of my heart. Urban living is our only choice for the moment, given Tom's job. He works on global health issues from his university office, focusing on poverty-stricken parts of the world where AIDS runs rampant. By supporting him in this work, I feel I'm doing something useful too—it's a family effort. But such reasonable thoughts did nothing to quell the downward spin of my brain. I soon became quite low-functioning, crying constantly and shaking uncontrollably, not eating, not sleeping, unable to get myself to do anything. I could almost hear Nurse Ratched following me around the house. And in spite of the nest being assembled just ten feet from the window of my sunny new study, I stopped studying crows.

"You are not having a nervous breakdown," Dr. Steffan told me. I huddled tearfully in a fluffy chair and looked sidelong at the first psychiatrist I'd seen in my life, which up until then had been remarkably peaceful. I wasn't? If this wasn't a nervous breakdown, what was? "Well, then, is this what depression is?" I asked. Hmm... he hesitated to call it that. Anxiety? He hesitated to call it that. Well *what?*

"Well," Dr. Steffan began to explain slowly, "there is a line—a good one—between seeing and feeling enough and seeing and feeling too much. Normally, we all keep well south of the latter line, and that serves us tolerably well in our daily interactions. You have lived your whole life closer to the line than is, um, normal. Or I should say *typical.* That is good—it is why you are"—he paused again—*"how you are.* A difficult way to be, but also beautiful sometimes, yes?"

I nodded pathetically. Difficult, beautiful, yes.

Dr. Steffan went on. "But living close to the line makes it easier to topple across it." I looked up. That's what happened? I toppled?

Some days I didn't get up in the morning. I peered over the top of the quilt, saw the sun beyond the Cascade mountains, sensed their beauty, but couldn't stop crying. I felt love and gratitude, and even a raw happiness when Tom and our nine-year-old daughter, Claire, came up to kiss me goodbye, but still I cried and shivered. Then they would leave, off to work and school, and I couldn't stand it. How could they have left? How could anyone leave me alone like this? And besides, what was that terrible sound?

It sounded like a baby crow cawing and cawing without pause. A young crow sounds very different from an adult, especially when it wants to—that is, whenever it's to her advantage to be seen as helpless and needy, to be seen as a young crow toward whom an adult crow might feel charitable and toss a crust of bread. I remembered it was midwinter, not baby crow season, rolled over, and shut my eyes. But this crow was insistent, and seemingly unheard by her target audience, whoever that might be. I started to wonder if the bird was in some sort of tormented danger—cornered by a cat, perhaps, or caught in the thorny branches of my merciless rosebush. Finally, I got out of bed and went to my study. There it was—a particularly disheveled-looking crow perched on the wire outside the window. The bird was just sitting there, being noisy, until she noticed me noticing her. And then she stopped, as if to say, "Ha! I got her out of bed," became silent, and turned her attention to a completely different task. She began to preen, vigorously, extensively, and at great length. She preened as if her skin was distressingly itchy and as if she was alarmed, and maybe even frightened, by the intensity of the discomfort. I assumed she must be plagued by one of the many ectoparasites that attack young crows, and I got out my spotting scope to see what I could; since the bird was only twelve feet away, and my scope could magnify to 80x, maybe I would be able to tell whether she was gathering anything in her bill. I noticed that she had a warty growth over one eye, probably an indication of avian pox, which sometimes affects crows. The growth might be painful, pressing into the oculus, I thought, and it certainly wasn't pretty. In a mood to be hyperaware of our interconnected frailty, I, naturally, started to cry. But I laughed, too, a tiny bit, seeing a blessed humor in my situation for the first time in months, standing there in my pink flannel pajamas, looking through a very expensive spotting scope at a common crow with a bad eye and a case of lice. Each of us, crow and human alike, was a disastrous, beautiful mess.

In spite of the chill air, I opened the two large windows wide and sat cross-legged on top of my desk in front of them. The crow stayed and preened. Without thinking, I picked up my notebook and sketched her from various angles. We both stayed there for two hours. I had a drawer full of crow studies—notebooks, observations, research, and musings. But that morning brought forth the most significant crow information I'd gleaned to date. Crows can get us out of bed. And they can do a lot more than that for us if we allow them.

I won't pretend an instantaneous cure, if *cure* is even the right word for a return to the lifelong effort to maintain a proper balance between beauty and difficulty with minimal toppling. It took many more days to get me out of my pajamas, and more days still to get me into my walking shoes. But once they were on my feet, my relationship to the crows around me changed; instead of being merely my current object of study, the crows became a liaison with a truer way of being, of more vitally, graciously, and intelligently inhabiting my urban home. The next months revealed to me that even though I'd always imagined myself to be a good urban ecologist—I recycled, walked and biked, gathered eggs from my backyard chicken coop, knew the names of birds and trees, collected signatures for environmental initiatives, and even taught classes in local natural history—I had resisted the idea of becoming a truly knowledgeable urban naturalist, feeling that this was just an impoverished version of a "real" naturalist. I'd saved my best thinking, my best watching, my best presence, and my bravest intimacy for true nature. But what exactly did I mean by *true nature?* And was this not a snobbish attitude? Am I really so much better than the place where I live? I, who am as much an introduced race as any Norway rat?

In his essay *Home Economics,* agrarian writer Wendell Berry defines nature this way: "What we call nature is, in a sense, the sum of the changes made by all the various creatures and natural forces in their intricate actions and influences upon each other and their places." In other words, for humans, *how* we live *where* we live is what makes us part of a natural ecosystem. It is also the source of our most profound impact on the more-than-human world.

We love our vision of untouched nature and cling tightly to images of pristine wilderness or desert or ocean as solace for our souls, as places of peace and transcendent beauty to which we can turn as a diversion from our cluttered, material lives. We believe ourselves to be intimately connected to wild places, as indeed we are. Too often, though, nature is romanticized as the place *out there,* the place with all the sparkly trees in the Sierra Club calendar, the place we visit with a knapsack and a Clif Bar, where we stand in awe of the beauty and refresh our spirits. But it is a kind of hubris to pretend that we come to such places unencumbered, that we can leave behind the snares, entanglements, and activities of our everyday lives and return to a kind of purity when we drive our SUVs (or even our hybrids) up to the hills for a subalpine-meadow hike, no matter how far we walk. Such sojourns are nourishing and necessary, but it remains our daily lives, in the places we live, that make us ecosystemic creatures; these are the seat of our most meaningful interactions with, and impact upon, the wider, wilder earth. We are connected by the ways that we choose, consume, and share water, food, shelter, and air—just like all the other animals. We cherish the few, sweet days we manage to escape to places we consider true wilderness, but the most essential things we can do for the deeply wild earth have to do with how we eat, how we drive, where we walk, and how we choose every moment of our quotidian urban lives.

When people—usually scientists or academics or nature writers—bother to define *nature,* one of two definitions typically emerges. Nature is either the whole of the physical world, excepting humans and their various constructs, or nature is the whole of the physical world, *including* humans and their various constructs. There is a portentous gap between these two definitions, but if we are going to consider our relationship to the more-than-human world with any kind of intelligence, it is a gap that we are going to have to navigate with some measure of sophistication.

I used to cling tightly to a chimeric vision of nature as something pure and somehow prehuman and to the idea that anything human-made removed a place from its natural status. But I have come to understand nature differently. Surely there is a continuum from a pure, undefiled wilderness to a trammeled concrete industrial area. But there is no place, we now know, as the relentlessly global impacts of climate change become increasingly understood, that humans have left untouched; and there is no place that the wild does not, in some small way, proclaim itself. Many human activities are wholly ugly, working against the nature upon which we forget we depend. Still, we do not flip-flop back and forth, now in nature, now in culture, now feeling quite animal-like, now wholly intellectual. We are, at all times, both at once. In this, humans may be unique, but we are no less natural. We are the human species, living in culture, bound by nature.

When we allow ourselves to think of nature as something out there, we become prey to complacency. If nature is somewhere else, then what we do here doesn't really matter. Jennifer Price writes in *Flight Maps,* her eloquent critique of romanticized nature, that modern Americans use an idea of Nature Out There to ignore our ravenous uses of natural resources. "If I don't think of a Volvo as nature, then can't I buy and drive it *to* Nature without thinking very hard about how I use, alter, destroy, and consume nature?" In my urban ecosystem, I drive around a corner and a crow leaps into flight from the grassy parking strip. We startle each other. If nature is Out There, she asks, then what am I?

To suggest that urban nature holds profound lessons is not to suggest that our concrete-laced wilds are, in any sense, adequate. Ecologically minded social critics are most often correct in proclaiming them to be impoverished places that incite a rampant consumerism, contriving at every moment to cut us off from any connection to a wilder earth. Urban sprawl—and the degraded, chopped–up habitat it leaves in its wake—is the single greatest threat to species diversity in the current millennium. If we wish to have a positive impact on the places we consider to be most profoundly wild, then we must begin by inhabiting our home ecosystems with some semblance of knowledge and grace.

Put on your walking shoes, my louse-ridden crow suggested. And I did. I took my daughter's hand and set out to drop the barriers I'd erected between my heart and my urban home. I would learn my place deeply and well, give the wild things that live here their due credit, and try to grasp how we might dwell together with intelligence, artistry, and joy. I would take my binoculars and sketchbook out of the field bag I carry when I visit nature *out there*, and drop them into the bag I carry every day, the one with my cell phone and my laptop and my bus pass. I would live as much in the presence of the wild as the urban landscape allows. I would learn, quickly, that this would be a creative challenge but not an impossible one. There are, after all, always crows.

Two

PREPARING

A Crash Course for the Urban Naturalist

We are human in good part because of the way we affiliate with other organisms. They are the matrix in which the human mind originated and is permanently rooted, and they offer the challenge and freedom innately sought. To the extent that each person can feel like a naturalist, the old excitement of the untrammeled world will be regained.

— E. O. WILSON

A couple of weeks after the lousy crow got me out of bed, I was driving Claire to school, when we passed a crow on the corner a couple of blocks from our house. It was pulling clumps of moss from the curb, then shaking them and picking at them with its bill. At the next corner, another crow was doing the same thing. I watched them for a minute until Claire said, "Mom, why aren't we going?" After dropping Claire off, I returned home and walked down the street with my binoculars and hand lens in search of the moss-plucking crows. Every curb I passed had piles of pulled-off moss beside it. Eventually I spotted a crow at one curb and found myself a witness to the sweeping spectrum of crow-beak coordination. The bird tore the moss off like a Neanderthal, then picked at it with forceps-like bill tips, as if doing brain surgery.

When I peeled some moss off to have a look myself, at first all I could see were moss, soil, and roots from the grass that grew throughout it. Nothing yummy, not even for a crow. But eventually I saw a tiny rice-size something that wriggled when I poked it — a larva of some kind — and then with effort I found several more. They barely looked like anything until I peered at them through my hand lens. At 10x magnification they became tiny lucent worlds — segmented, multiple shades of gray, and very busy. They seemed awfully small for a crow to bother with, but I decided this must be what they were eating. I was freezing my tookas off, picking through wet moss in January, so I brought some home, dumped it on a plate, and continued studying the larvae, accompanied by Delilah, our cat. After flipping through a botanical guidebook, I eventually identified the moss as *Tortula muralis,* which, though mosses are notoriously difficult to identify, is not that impressive a thing to have done; it is one of the most common mosses on earth, growing happily on urban concrete. It is the crow of mosses.

I called an entomologist friend, who told me that although the little larvae could be many things, cane flies lay their eggs in mossy debris, usually in lawns, but conceivably along curbs. Cane fly larvae would be larger than my minute specimens, and perhaps worth searching for by hungry crows, but he suggested that maybe the birds were looking for cane fly larvae and taking whatever else they could find. This was plausible. But why didn't I see crows doing this a couple of weeks ago? "Oh," he told me, "the larvae don't really emerge until February." "But it's only January," I said. "*End* of January," he reminded me. "Yeah, well, global warming, you know."

I looked back at my saucer full of moss, still on the surface and squirming beneath. Insects so tiny I could barely see them without my hand lens had emerged, jumping and scrambling about the slippery plate. Here was a whole ecosystem reflected in a bit of sidewalk moss, from decomposing leaves to feasting avian omnivores. Sometimes the extent of unseen life makes my head spin so hard I actually feel nauseated. I carried the moss and its denizens outside and tucked them back on their curb. Philosopher Alfred North Whitehead wrote, "It requires a very unusual mind to undertake the analysis of the obvious." Nausea or no, I suppose this is the mind the urban naturalist is called to cultivate.

Developing as a naturalist, a knower of nature, is arguably one of the most critical tasks for modern humans on the planet Earth, yet *naturalist* is a word and a role that has, in the last century, lost its core meaning. Not that the term isn't used. After about half a millennium during which the title was deemed archaic and dropped out of common parlance, *naturalist* is suddenly the word of the moment. It seems everyone calls herself a naturalist these days. The counselors who watch over my daughter at day camp? Naturalists. "Why are they called naturalists?" I inquired of the camp director. Well, because of all the nature activities, of course. And it's true that my daughter did bring home a mosaic fashioned of leaves and sticks glued onto a paper plate. Claire and the other fifty children also pillaged the native plants around a nearby pond and stuffed them into ill-fated mayonnaise-jar terrariums that sat on kitchen counters for two weeks, all fogged up, before dying. The high school student at the city aquarium who, bless her, memorized all twelve species in the "touch-tank" and spends her summer helping children identify them is distinguished as a naturalist on her name tag. It seems anyone connected with any sort of job that can be construed as having something to do with nature becomes, on their résumé, a naturalist. But knowing a little something about nature, while good, does not make someone a naturalist. This is a beautiful title, worth reclaiming.

The naturalist tradition has its roots in the human tendency to seek order in nature. Aristotle is often recognized as the first naturalist in the Western scientific tradition, and though there were surely capable observers and thinkers in the natural world before him, it is his two-thousand-year-old writings that have endured. In his *History of Animals,* Aristotle stressed the absolute significance of personal, direct observation in the study of nature, and he compiled an impressive catalog of information based on his own inquiries. Studying the animals around him, and particularly birds, Aristotle articulated the first known species concept in his idea of "natural kinds," animals and plants that share particular qualities and so can be distinguished from others. He also spun some fantastic theories, including the notion that the redstarts that disappeared from the Greek Isles each fall actually transmogrified into the robins that appeared to replace them (and later turned back into redstarts again).

Since Aristotle lacked even dim knowledge of avian migration, this wasn't really bad natural history, based as it was in honest observation of living things. Aristotle never attempted a sensible means of classifying or understanding the relationships between organisms, but his work inspired the later efforts of Linnaeus and Buffon in the 1700s.

Believing that it was his great work as a natural historian to create a comprehensive "catalog of life," Carolus Linnaeus devised the first serious botanical classification system, relying on similar characteristics between organisms to place them in sensible groups. His system is too simple, and also botanically inaccurate, to be of use today, but his binomial nomenclature, in which every organism is named by its genus and species with a pair of Latinized names that are recognized by all scientists, is of enduring value (born Carl von Linné, Linnaeus even Latinized his own name). Georges-Louis Leclerc, Comte de Buffon, Linnaeus's contemporary and sometime-nemesis, believed classification to be of secondary importance. For him, the goal of natural history was to reveal the broad order of nature, where there was much more at stake than the listing of discrete organisms. For Buffon, the natural historian's proper role involved the study of the relationships between creatures, their geological substrate, the patterns of weather, the movements of history, and the grand interplay of all these things.

Both Linnaeus and Buffon resisted Aristotle's mandate to observe with one's own eyes; rather than firsthand research in the field, they relied mainly on large specimen collections. In this, their work fed the Cabinet of Wonders

craze that began in the eighteenth century and blossomed in
the first half of the nineteenth, in which every respectable
middle- or upper-class household boasted a display of natural curiosities, and museums were little more than glorified
arrangements of specimens. A Cabinet of Wonders sounds
like a marvelous, imaginative thing, and many of them were
exceedingly beautiful, but most often, even in museums,
they were simply an aesthetically arranged jumble of dead
things, with little pretense to naturalistic truth or educational value. The "naturalists" of this time were often little
more than specimen collectors, dispatched around the globe
to pillage the flora and fauna for the enjoyment of rich Euro-
peans. (In the interest of full disclosure, I should mention
that we maintain our own little Cabinet of Wonders in our
living room. It contains evidence of our natural surround-
ings and wanderings: the skulls of a Western Grebe and an
Evening Grosbeak; a warthog tusk and a flamingo feather
from our trip to Kenya; the cast of a tiny pteranodon fossil;
as well as various stones, feathers, desiccated insects, shells,
and other news from the universe that rotates seasonally
through. We try to look at these things, not as disembodied
trinkets, but as a complement—by way of inspiration and
reminder—to our family nature study. Unlike the displays
in eighteenth- and nineteenth-century parlors, though, I fear
this one does little for my social standing. Visiting children
are terrifically interested, but their mothers often whisper
reservedly, "Oh, I see you have *skulls*.")

Even with the cabinet fad in full bloom, it was the
early nineteenth century that brought the study of natural

history—the study of organisms in their places—back onto its own lovely footing. Students who were drawn to science through a love of wild nature began to combine direct, in situ study of organisms with judicious use of museum collections in the creation of broader theories. Charles Darwin's nuanced understanding of evolution through natural selection was drawn almost entirely from his own relatively simple observations of animals in their places. These days, when academic specialization in the sciences has overtaken the work of describing, naming, classifying, and understanding organisms, natural history is rarely taken seriously as a scientific discipline and is seen as more of a hobby, relegated to amateurs and "bird-watchers." But there are inspiring exceptions. The chemical biologist Thomas Eisner at Cornell teaches a course called The Naturalist's Way, where the mind-set and methods of the naturalist's way of knowing are explored in depth and across disciplines. Eisner's good friend the Pulitzer Prize–winning scientist E. O. Wilson insists that global identification of individual species is a necessary groundwork for conservation; the naturalist's ability to knowingly discern species is foundational to this effort.

It's interesting that books about historical naturalists almost always follow this short outline: from Aristotle to Darwin, and perhaps wrapping up with the example of a modern scientist-naturalist, typically Wilson. The place of the lay naturalist, working outside of academic science, is rarely considered. But I believe that the two histories can hardly be disentangled. From the time of Linnaeus and surely before, women and men with no official scientific credentials but

with an affinity for the natural world have, through dedicated self-education, influenced our understanding of earthly
life, and our place within it. Born in the late 1800s, one of
my personal heroines, Margaret Morse Nice, wrote in her
autobiography about the moment when she realized that the
study of nature could lift her above her life as a housewife
and mother, a life that she found benumbing but beyond
which she was not socially expected to tread:

> Under the great elms and cottonwoods on the river
> bank I watched the turbulent Canadian River and
> dreamed. The glory of nature possessed me. I saw
> that for many years I had lost my way. I had been
> led astray on false trails and had been trying to do
> things contrary to my nature. I resolved to return to
> my childhood vision of studying nature and trying
> to protect the wild things of the earth.

Nice's extensive studies of Song Sparrow breeding and
nesting habits eventually gained her world fame as a field
biologist and the praise of scientific thinkers such as Kon-
rad Lorenz and Ernst Mayr. Nice's monographs and essays
inspired a generation of lay naturalists after her, many of
them women, who had not previously dreamed that their
own personal observations had value. These are the men
and women who would form the first generation of naturalist organizations, including the Audubon Naturalist Society (as the modern Audubon Society was first named), that
were scientifically informed, believed in the potential of lay

individuals to develop as competent students of nature, and bent an eye toward conservation of wild places. These individuals and early groups serve as inspiration for the modern urban naturalist, who as a starting point might find herself, in Nice's words, "led astray on false trails."

To my mind, a contemporary naturalist is a person who studies deeply, richly, seriously, and over a respectable swath of time, the life and ecology of a chosen place or places. *Naturalist* is a liberal arts title, and it might involve philosophy, literature, art, and an expansive sense of spirit as much as it does science. This is absolutely not to say that we ought to lapse into some murky New Age condition in which we become one with nature at the level of the heart and avoid the "cold" academics of science. Not at all. Rather, the amateur naturalist is in the wonderful position of being both scientifically informed and unencumbered by the restrictive parameters of traditional scientific reporting (statistical significance, aversion to anecdote, and so on). As naturalists, we can fill our notebooks with anything that the breadth of nature can dream up and give us. Anything true. Anything that we are present and attentive enough to witness.

In the modern urban setting, the naturalist's way suggests an antidote to the overinfluence of specialization upon our everyday lives. Today we leave our health to doctors, our food to agribusiness, and our knowledge of the biological realm to information received from scientists. Such specialization, writes author Michael Pollan, "obscures lines of connection—and responsibility." The foundational knowledge unearthed by modern naturalists is simultaneously

freeing, consoling, and revolutionary. So often it is the amateur naturalists in a community who spearhead grassroots
projects to protect local, wild places and their denizens. We
can take responsibility for our own biological education, and
the earth-sustaining work it entails need not wait for anoint-
ing from either academia or politicians.

Over the past decade I have thought and written a fair bit
about the role of the naturalist—the importance of the naturalist's attitude both for oneself and for the conservation of
earthly life. I believe strongly that effective and lasting conservation efforts are based in an everyday awareness of our
continuity with the more-than-human world, an awareness
that is cultivated through study and observation. Still, bringing this sensibility to my daily urban life has posed an unexpectedly steep challenge. My images of what is and what
is not nature, what is and what is not worthy of the kind of
attunement that characterizes the naturalist's way of seeing,
are more deeply ingrained than I even guessed. I quickly
discovered that just declaring myself to be an aspiring urban
naturalist was not enough. I didn't believe myself.

Wondering how to realize this shift, I decided to start
by imitating the way I would wander into a place that I did
deem worthy of my careful attention. Regrettably, I came
to see that this meant just one thing. Since I am a commit-
ted student of birdlife, I would never dream of walking a
woodland pathway or a riverbank or a sweep of Puget Sound

shoreline without my binoculars. Now I had declared the sidewalk my path. That meant I had to carry my binoculars everywhere.

For me, this was not as much of a stretch as it would be for some. I usually do have binoculars with me, and I even keep a spotting scope in the car. And of course we always have a pair on the kitchen table, which overlooks the backyard, so as a family we can keep track of the finches, wrens, migrant warblers, and sundry creatures that might at any moment grace our home life. But it was not my practice to carry binoculars when I went on my daily neighborhood walks. I did not carry them into the cafés where I often sit by a window writing, sometimes wondering what that bird is just beyond my normal visual capacity. I did not carry them when I walked to the grocery store, the fruit stand, or Target. But now I resolved to carry them to all of these places, and everyplace else besides. I would wander everywhere as I wander in the forest — ready to see.

Surely wearing binoculars is a novel fashion statement, one that has yet to be discovered by Paris, New York, or even Seattle, where we regularly dine out in polar fleece and wear sweat socks with our sandals. Carrying binoculars around my neck, I have been stared at, asked (many times) what I am doing, questioned by police, and whispered over by teenagers ("*Nice* binoculars," is the typical, deadpan comment).

With binoculars in place, it takes only the addition of a notebook and pencil to turn a purse or a laptop computer satchel into a field bag. In my own bag, I now carry my wallet, my lipstick (which I pretend that I don't wear but actually do), my notebook and pencil (I admit to taking notes on the fancy sort of paper that takes lead and ink when soaking wet—a useful extravagance in the Pacific Northwest), and my thermal coffee mug (in Seattle one is rarely more than a few hundred yards from rich, dark, organic, shade-grown java).

I also carry a small luxury: my beautiful little Swift 10x magnification hand lens, which was a gift from my sister more than twenty years ago. Somehow I have managed to avoid losing its tiny leather case, and I keep it hanging around my neck like jewelry by a weathered cord adorned with beads I've picked up in Santa Fe, Japan, and India, along with a special protective bead that a graduate school friend brought back from Africa—just in case I meet some particularly terrible crows, I guess. I use the hand lens all the time to examine such things as plant stems, mosses, mushroom caps, spiders in their webs, bits of bone and feather, and the contents of crow or gull pellets. If we are ready for them, small, beautiful things that bear magnification turn up regularly.

The only truly essential items in my bag are the notebook and pencil. Though I am attached to my binoculars and all that they imply, a person could start off without them, especially with crows as a subject. This is one way that crows are rare as birds go: they can be watched reasonably well without optics.

It may not seem particularly imaginative to compile a list of naturalist qualities, habits that seem to be exhibited across the board by the best students of nature, but I have found that regarding the ways and roles of the naturalist, certain practices emerge over and over. Putting them down here I am reminded afresh of what I have learned and what I have yet to fully grasp. My intent was to revise notes I had made earlier on the "outer-wilds" naturalist, making them relevant for this new project of bringing naturalist practices into my daily urban life. But I was struck by how little revision was needed, how the naturalist's tendencies traverse any terrain our feet can drag us over. It is a good list and still, I am sure, an incomplete one, distilled from my own experiences of watching everything from black bears and Northern Goshawks in places we would traditionally consider to be the fabulously true wild, to the hobo spider in the corner of my living room with the heap of unidentified insect corpses beneath her web. These practices are drawn from my field notebooks, from my reading, and, especially, from lurking attentively in the presence of people who are much better naturalists than I will ever be, gleaning hints from the books they have penned, their conversation, and their habits in the field. These are the habits I hope to cultivate and carry into my dotage, the ways I want to model for my daughter.

Study. It is romantic to think that if we venture forth with nothing but a sense of hopeful willingness, we will see wondrous things. This is to some extent true, but we will see fewer of them if we have not spent some time with field guides or other literature about our home ecosystems. Louis Pasteur famously commented that "chance favors the prepared mind," a maxim that proves almost magically true time and again.

Recently I decided that I was pathetically ill-informed about local non-butterfly insects, so I purchased a book on the insects of the Pacific Northwest. At any time of day, I am hardly more than a few feet from an insect or some other arthropod that I have never seen and about which I know nothing. I'll unearth a shining larva while gardening, call Claire over to see it, and when the tip starts to wiggle, I'll scream like a schoolgirl.

Studying the book as a family, we chose to begin with the spider section. (Spiders are not insects, of course; as even preschoolers these days enjoy pointing out, spiders are arachnids, but the author of my book helpfully included sections on spiders, millipedes, and other greater-than-six-legged creatures that we might chance upon.) Claire knows our household spiders freakishly well. She names them all: currently we have Abigail behind the front door, Puddles in the bathroom, and a wandering Fiona. Claire monitors their webs, diagrams their whereabouts, and worries over their diets. She wonders whether it is ethical to toss an insect Abigail's way if it seems none are finding their way to her web themselves. She puts up notes to reroute guests if their ramblings might disturb one of our arachnid roommates. She knows our household spiders every bit as well as I know the neighborhood crows, and I'm impressed with her studies.

On our first night looking at the new book, we marveled over the photo and description of the *Argiope aurantia*, the

Black and Yellow Argiope spider, common throughout the United States. And the very next day, for the first time ever, we found a wriggling cluster of freshly emerged argiope spiderlings under the lowest wooden step of our back deck. While Claire hovered over the spiderlings and sketched them in her notebook, I wondered over the fact that if we'd found these spiders just the day before, we would have known nothing about them. And I was sure, on some level, that it was learning about them that allowed us to find them. Whenever I renew a commitment to studying raptors or gulls or crows or the birds in my backyard, more are given, more show themselves. Our efforts are rewarded, our studies are enhanced in experience. I cannot explain this, and I am reluctant to sound too woo-woo but we can take this as confidently as if it came from the Oracle at Delphi: the more we prepare, the more we are "allowed" somehow to see. This is a guarantee: select a subject, obtain a proper field guide, study it well, and you will see more than you ever have of your chosen subject—and more than that besides.

Name Things. Naming is a skill that follows from study. There are sensitive, poetic people who believe that the human scientific obsession with naming other animals shows a kind of arrogance, an imposition of our limited human sensibility upon creatures who have no use for our overconfident proclamations about their kind and status. I understand the impulse to resist the complete human intellectual colonization of the nonhuman world, but surely our desire to name organisms can be seen in another light. Knowing the name of a creature is a window into knowing much more—its relationship to other similar creatures, its ecological place, its body, its diet, its dwelling. In his memoir, E. O. Wilson recalls that as a young student of biology at the University of Alabama, his mentor required him to learn the scientific names of ten thousand organisms before he could begin to think of himself as a naturalist. At first I thought that seemed an impractical goal for a modern, urban-dwelling, mom-writer-naturalist. But now I think, "Why not?" Why not learn the names of ten thousand organisms, gathering them like shells until my brain swells with the weight of such unusual knowledge? And why not get busy with it right away? Even then I would be only scratching the dim, light surface of the earth's wild diversity.

Beginners might quickly become overwhelmed, trying to learn the name of every plant, insect, spider, and bird whose path they cross, in which case, it is good to choose a class of beings with which to start. Birds are a good choice for a number of reasons: because they are so present and lovely; because, bearing wings, they appeal simultaneously to our scientific and poetic sensibilities, because compared with plants or insects they are reasonably limited in number; and because there are so many good and complete field guides for just about any geographical region. Nonvertebrates, be they beach dwellers or backyard insects, are more formidable; there is such a shocking number of them and they are less familiar, not having bones, like us.

At the very least, it is satisfying to know the basic biota of our home place—the names of the most prominent native trees and plants, twenty or thirty of the species of birds and their seasonal patterns, the mammals present (whether they show themselves or not), and, depending on where we live and what we are most likely to see, perhaps also a few reptiles, insects, and mushrooms. This naming can effect a tremendous psychological difference in our sense of home and community. Names have meaning beyond themselves, carrying, curiously, more weight than other words do. It is like the difference between knowing and not knowing our neighbors' names. But of course the name of an organism is just the first thing we know and hopefully not, ultimately, the only thing.

Practice and Have Patience. When we set out, we might feel prepared, carrying our field guides and perhaps binoculars. We might feel possessed of simultaneous enthusiasm and patience. We are, after all, translators of a new vision, stepping forth into a world that suddenly looks...the same. Damn. No matter how urgently we page through our field guides, listen for wisps of avian song, seek the droppings by which we might analyze a passing bird's diet, or look for tracks in the roadside mud, the lack of news from the wild can make us feel distressingly stupid. We learn quickly that the guide and the field are two different things; the journey from tidy diagram to disheveled bird is as perilous as it is joyful. But surely there is some good in this feeling—it means we are acquiring new skills, however slowly. With patience and practice, we will have to work harder for evidence of our own edifying ignorance (but fear not—it will never leave us).

Respect the Wildness of Animals. Learning to respect a wild being's "otherness" is a tricky lesson. So much of our work as naturalists draws us rightly into a sense of connection, and yet now we are being asked to understand simultaneously that it is not an act of respect to think that we are one with the animals that we observe, that they love us, or that we are their friends. They would in nearly all cases prefer that we go away. I am not talking about maintaining a pristine scientific distance, nor could I credibly do so (I often find myself unwittingly talking to birds, trees, and mushrooms; Claire and I have named every crab on the beach; and though I know how much it must frighten them, I like to scoop up newts and stroke their flat, sleepy-eyed little heads). I am talking, rather, about being aware of ourselves as watchers and, when it matters, paying attention to the line between intimate observation and overstepping. It takes only a bit of experience and common sense to notice when our presence has disturbed a wild animal, and to realize that we can hardly study an animal's behavior if we have shocked it into witless stillness or chased it away. The boundary between edifying closeness and harmful disturbance is not drawn plainly; it changes according to circumstance and the organisms being observed. Pestering a crow has little ecological consequence. Forcing a flock of migratory shorebirds into flight causes them to expend the precious energy they are gathering as they feed along the shore and may contribute to the difference between a bird's successful migration across the ocean and its falling out of the sky to a watery death. Far less dramatically, we can disturb plants, lichens, seastars, and barnacles, though of course they offer far fewer behavioral clues than most animals. We watch where we step.

Cultivate an Obsession. While most good students of natural history are observant of life around them generally, it is also beneficial to always be working with a specific question in mind—a particular group, species, or issue upon which you lavish thought, study, and attention. Darwin and Thoreau are among the famous obsessors who knew that a good question fills us with a sense of purpose and gives structure to our observations. It engages our mind on levels unforeseen. It leads to more knowledge than hapless wandering about can, and rather than narrowing the creative response, it seems, somehow, to mysteriously expand it. Questions lead to further questions, and inquiry breeds insight. Gathering expertise brings both confidence and consolation. E. O. Wilson wrote: "You start by loving a subject. Birds, probability theory, stars, differential equations, storm fronts, sign language, swallowtail butterflies.... The subject will be your lodestar and give sanctuary in the shifting mental universe."

Carry a Notebook. Writing is a way of seeing. Writing catches a moment and lends it substance. Writing down an observation gives us a sense of, and a trust in, our vision. It helps us to realize that a crow stepping over a rock, or turning its head forty-five degrees so it can eye us at an angle, or urgently preening the feathers about the neck, is *something*. Something we have now seen, a world we have now entered, but one that is always, always there, even without us. We remember that we were made for this knowledge. E. O. Wilson has written extensively of biophilia—the innate human tendency to know and love the natural, wild earth, and the further sense that this knowing is part of our health, our imagination, and our intelligence. In the habit of writing down our observations, however messily, sketchily, or dreamily, we unearth and indulge this love.

Mind the Gadgetry. The binocular-carrying practice has taught me the extent to which my sense of purpose is curiously linked to what I'm carrying. Perhaps it is akin to the psychology around costume wearing: when we don a gown or wig for Halloween, we mysteriously take on new postures and gestures. Just as it is helpful to carry the few things that outfit us for awareness, it is equally worthwhile to avoid the superfluous. The other day I paged through a prominent yoga magazine that was full of advertisements for consumer goods a person might need to be a good yogini. Special socks, books, arts, clocks, and jewelry. The most ironic headline read "Stuff for Your Spiritual Life." I've found that the ads in bird and nature magazines are really no better. They are full of things we are increasingly made to feel we need in order to be a proper watcher. Expensive optics, for starters—better than the ones we have (regardless of what those may be), ergonomically designed, preferably in Czechoslovakia, and for the price of a small home in India. We need recording devices, cameras, and computer programs that will allow us to identify birds in the field with awe-inspiring efficiency. These last we are to install on the laptops that we *carry with us*, and that really don't weigh that much more than a field guide, we are told (assuming, it seems, that the field guide is a big one). And while we're about it, we'd better buy a vest with pockets specially designed to hold all this stuff we need to carry. Long before laptops, the philosopher Jean-Jacques Rousseau claimed, "The more ingenious and accurate our instruments, the more unsusceptible and inexpert become our organs: by assembling a heap of machinery about us, we find afterwards none in ourselves." This commodification of watching is a falsehood, and a terrible loss. The plain, subversive, radical truth is that we do not need to go shopping in order to watch birds. In its pure simplicity, observation of nature may be the most countercultural thing an ecologically minded person can do.

Maintain a "Field Trip" Mentality. Joining a field trip of birders is like falling through the looking glass. For hours on end you are thrown into a parallel universe with people who have nothing on their minds except finding and watching birds, and who know a great deal about how to do both of these things. The field trip starts immediately, right at the car, before you divide into carpools and head off to the destination. Everyone arrives with binoculars already out of the case and around their necks. Everyone is seeing, pointing, naming, flipping through field guides. The finding and naming and watching last all day, no matter how "good" or "bad" the birding, or how terrible the weather. Only when the sun is setting, and everyone is frozen and hungry, do the hard-core watchers come in from the cold deck of the ferry boat returning to Seattle across Puget Sound, pointing and exclaiming. By now, I would normally have huddled on a ferry seat, wrapped myself in polar fleece, poured some coffee from my thermos, and begun wondering in earnest whether I would ever regain feeling in my cold-numbed toes. "Did you see anything?" I ask the wild watchers when they finally come inside. "No," they reply and smile broadly, and with such pure, giddy happiness that I wonder briefly whether they have lost their sanity.

The take-home lesson is one of mind-set. With my new habit of carrying binoculars everywhere, I feel imbued with a readiness to see, an attitude that my life itself is a kind of field trip. The urban naturalist has the terrific luxury of stepping out her door and into "the field," without long rides or carpools, or putting money in for gas and Dairy Queen. When does the field trip begin? Whenever we start paying attention.

Make Time for Solitude. This is every bit as true as it is a cliché. While we can learn much with others, we watch differently, and essentially, when alone.

Stand in Lineage, and with a Sense of Purpose. In Victorian times, a fairly deep study of natural history was not unusual, and while there were academic naturalists, ordinary people also studied the natural world for self-edification or social distinction. In a time of ecological crisis, the place of the naturalist has become necessarily multifaceted. Naturalists are people who know what's going on. They know what creatures live where, which are thriving and why, and which are dying and why. They know their earthen places well and can, by example and action, speak eloquently for their ecological needs. Modern naturalists must be both biologically and politically savvy, which can be a rude awakening. How nice it would be to just watch warblers and make little yellow watercolors of them in our notebooks. But I believe strongly that the modern naturalist's calling includes an element of activism. Naturalists are witnesses to the wild, and necessary bridges between ecological and political ways of knowing. When Rachel Carson began work on *Silent Spring* in the late 1950s, she was already the acclaimed author of three books on the sea. Her beloved friend Dorothy Freeman objected to the new "poison" book, believing the subject matter was too negative and dark. In a letter to Freeman, Carson wrote, "You do know, I think, how deeply I believe in the importance of what I am doing. Knowing what I do, there would be no future peace for me if I kept silent." As we work to know the life that surrounds us, we stand in a lineage of naturalists—past, present, and even future. We join the "cloud of witnesses" who refuse to let the more-than-human world pass unnoticed.

I want to cocreate and inhabit a nation of watchers, of naturalists-in-progress, none of us perfect, all sharing in the effort of watching, knowing, understanding, protecting, and living well alongside the wild life with whom we share our cities, our neighborhoods, our households, our yards, our ecosystems, our earth. All of us in cafés, pulling out our laptops and beside them our binoculars, just in case we want to see how that crow outside the window is doing with his bit of garbage, how his feet work to hold down the paper bag while his nimble bill extracts the french fries. Just in case we want to see, above the crows, the swooping swallows that only days ago arrived all the way from Mexico, violet feathers shimmering. From the swallows we can turn to the person at the table across the way and say, "Did you ever see a more beautiful color of blue?"

Three

READING

CROW STORIES AND ANIMAL ALPHABETS

Story telling is the most ancient form of education. It is about the remembering, making, and sharing of images that bind together time, nature, and people. Stories, like the sacred plants, are medicine and food come from the Earth. They remind us that we do not stand alone. Through them we live in the body of coyote and crow, tree and stone. . . . In this way, we confirm our relationship with all of creation.

— JOAN HALIFAX

L ate this winter, we had the most astonishing hailstorm I have ever witnessed. There was so much hail I could not even see across the street, and it was so loud and beat down so hard that the entire house rattled. I opened the windows of my study and sat up on my desk. To my complete surprise, a crow flew up and landed on the big cypress outside my window. Instead of settling on a sheltered inner branch, this crow chose to perch on an outer branch, one being pelted so hard by hail that it quaked. She shivered her wings and looked up. As the hail beat down on her face, she opened her mouth and sat very still, as if in contemplative rapture. There she stayed until the hail began to fall more lightly, at which point she brought her head back in line, looked all around at the freshly hailed world, shook out her feathers, and flew to the very top of the Douglas fir down the block, where three other crows appeared to be enjoying the hailstorm. This was all very curious and *just like crows,* I thought, to revel in hail. I reached for my notebook to write this all down but then remembered. Hadn't I read something about crows and hail? Yes, there it was, clearly stated in Catharine Feher-Elston's *Ravensong:* "Crows are afraid of hail."

This is what crow watching is like. One contradiction after another. One act of outright defiance against the "crow literature" after another. The ornithological commentaries that turn up in the bulk of the peer-reviewed journals are constrained by the typical scientific admonitions: studies must be both quantifiable and replicable; they must not resort to anecdote; and they must not — god forbid! — anthropomorphize their subject. A very great deal of what crows do can be made to fit within these strictures. Crows share certain calls that occur in particular circumstances, have common social customs, and make nests out of roughly the same materials and in the same shape. We can write long treatises about American Crow morphology, behavior, breeding, and diet that will be pretty much true for most individuals of the species. But there is another aspect of crow life, the one that brings the rather dull crow of science to fabulous life as the crow on our sidewalk.

Unlike the crow in the ornithological journal, the crow outside our window indulges in a shocking array of behaviors that could only be called anecdotal: they happened, we saw them, and we made them real in telling the tale. We cannot prove what we saw, because it is unlikely that we will find a crow doing the exact same thing ever again. These are the crow stories that entwine our lives like vines.

Everybody has a crow story. I heard of a crow who accompanied a mail carrier on his daily route every day for more than two years, walking behind him like a golden retriever before inexplicably disappearing. I heard from a Benedictine nun that a crow in the woods surrounding her monastery befriended a large black, green-eyed cat named Ashford, and that the two shared in feasting on the birds that Ashford caught and killed. I just heard from a friend that she was watching a crow work for some time to balance a medium-size stone atop a larger stone. "Was it making art?" she wanted to know. I heard from a pilot friend that *his* friend (for many crow stories spiral compellingly through some kind of lineage in this way), also a pilot, watched the Snowbirds (the Canadian Forces' equivalent of the Blue Angels) practicing for an air show, and afterward, a crow in the trees near the airfield practiced flying upside down. Am I incredulous? Certainly, somewhat. But can I deny it? Who hasn't seen a crow do something we do not expect of "simple" birds, or any animal for that matter? Who doesn't have a crow story? And the more attention we offer, the more the crow stories spring up around us, like grass.

Crows are immensely intelligent, which is the main reason that their behaviors are so complex, unpredictable, fascinating, and mystifying. No matter what one's personal opinion of crows may be, almost everyone agrees that they are exceedingly clever. It is difficult to look at a crow and keep from thinking that it is thinking something itself, and there is every reason to believe that this is so. (*What* crows are thinking is another order of question altogether.) In both the scientific community and the public, there has been general agreement for decades—perhaps millennia—that corvids are an intelligent avian group. Even so, we have yet to fully transcend the cultural inheritance regarding avian intelligence imposed by the traditional phylogenetic scale. In the nineteenth century, German neuroanatomist Ludwig Edinger overlaid Darwin's branching tree of life with Aristotle's early *scala natura*, suggesting an evolutionary progression in life forms from lower to higher (not Darwin's intent). Thus, according to Edinger we have insects below fish, and fish below birds, and birds below mammals generally, and mammals generally below the higher mammals (apes), and apes below evolution's supposed pinnacle—humans. Even though modern science has proven that such a scale does not reflect evolutionary truth, it remains a cultural given that there are higher and lower vertebrates. Birds are almost invariably grouped among the lower. (We make allowances for the birds we know as pets, and African Gray parrots are considered a flagship example of avian intelligence, rivaling that of primates. John Paul Barret, who raised several young crows in Oregon, wrote, "They made our African Grays look like morons.")

In a recent paper published in *Science,* animal behaviorists Nathan Emery and Nicola Clayton at Cambridge University consolidated various studies indicating that the mentality of crows is very similar to that of apes. They looked at a range of behaviors exhibited by crows and other corvids and concluded that crows and apes have basically the same "cognitive toolbox," which evolved in response to similar social and ecological challenges. They described four cognitive pathways employed by both groups that suggest complex mentation: *causal reasoning* (as in the development and use of tools); *flexibility* (one of the "cornerstones of intelligent behavior," which refers to the ability to generate rules from past experiences that offer a varied repertoire of potential responses to novel stimuli, rather than simple "rote" learning, which seems to be the cognitive limit in some other avian groups, such as pigeons); *imagination* (where situations and scenarios not presently available can still be formed in the "mind's eye"); and *prospection* (the ability to imagine future events). We can see crows employing various combinations of these cognitive traits, such as when they soak dried bread in our birdbaths to soften it before eating; when they drop nuts or shells onto the road and wait for a car to run over them so they can reach the meat inside; when they deceive us as to the whereabouts of their nests, flying to one tree with their stick if they see us watching them, when their nest is actually in another tree; or when they poke holes in plastic grocery bags to see if there's any food inside. Betty, the New Caledonian Crow made famous on YouTube, demonstrated keen causal reasoning as she quickly formed a piece of wire into a hook to retrieve food from a cylinder. Emery and Clayton's work gives a scientific basis to what has seemed obvious to observers of crow-family birds for decades — crows are really smart.

Crows often engage in behaviors that we have traditionally ascribed only to so-called higher animal groups, those
with the most advanced intelligence and social systems,
and ornithologists have sometimes been reluctant, at least
in print, to interpret these behaviors as indicators of complex consciousness. That is just not how we talk about birds.
Crows sometimes take care of one another when injured,
for example. When we see a small group of crows huddled
on the side of the road and they seem not to be busy with
foraging, it may be that a member of their family is wounded
and is being tended by the others. Last autumn I stopped
to check on one such group, and in fact a young, very thin
bird, hatched that spring, was broken-winged, probably from
being hit by a car. Examining the bird, I could feel her keel, or
breastbone, protruding sharply through what ought to have
been a nice fat breast. Green excrement pasted around her
vent indicated dehydration. The four crows that had been
gathered around scattered into the near bushes, but they
watched while I looked the young bird over. Curiously, they
were quiet, neither scolding nor mobbing me. This little bird
was going to die, sooner rather than later. I thought about
taking her with me to euthanize her (rather than wringing
her neck in front of the other crows, which would upset them
terribly, not to mention me). But I decided to leave her there
with the crows that were obviously watching and feeding it.
Caring for her, really, is the proper word. I drove about five
hundred yards down the road and got out of the car with my
binoculars to watch. The crows gathered about the injured
bird once more and just sat there with her quietly. This was a

crow hospice, and it seemed the attendant birds were simply "being with" the dying crow, just as we are asked by human hospice workers to be present to our own beloved dying. This was a sweet, arresting moment to witness, and I have since seen other instances of crows gathering with attentive care around sick or injured birds, and friends have described similar scenes.

There are more ways that crows take care of one another. Obviously they are good parents, feeding and protecting their young, as could be said of any bird and nearly any animal. But in some of the ways they spend their time together, crows are again more like the animals we consider most intelligent, primates such as chimps and gorillas. Mutual grooming, or allopreening, is one of the best examples. Two crows huddle together, and one of them combs the other carefully with its bill, preening the feathers and picking ectoparasites from the skin. Young birds are preened by their parents, mates allopreen, and the sickly or the weak seem to get an extra dose of preening by those birds for whom they are in the circle of concern. Charlotte was preened by an adult bird for nearly a year after her hatching, months longer than her sibling. Crows being preened put their heads down to provide better access to the backs of their necks, where the scratching must feel extra good, much like dogs offer their bellies, and humans their backs. The benefits of allopreening are both physical and social—solidifying and deepening intra-crow relationships, and maybe picking a few nits in the process.

Betty is not the only crow who knows how to use tools,

though her fashioning of a hook from wire is particularly impressive. American Crows have often been observed making use of objects for their own purposes. Oklahoma State University zoologist and crow researcher Carolee Caffrey observed a female crow that she had color-banded swoop down on a student who was climbing a tree to examine the bird's nest. After a couple of dives, the crow dislodged a cone from the tree and dropped it on the student's head. She repeated the process twice more, making her mark each time. Caffrey has also documented a crow that was trying to reach down into a hole in a rotting fence. Using its feet and bill, the crow dislodged a sliver of wood from the fence, then removed splinters from the end of the wood fragment to make it narrower. It then poked this "tool" into the hole repeatedly, but eventually gave up, dropped the wood, and left. Caffrey later found a spider crouched deep inside the hole, apparently just out of reach. Many of us have probably seen crows engage objects for play. They enjoy dropping sticks in flight and then catching them in their bills. They drop things on one another—sticks, leaves, flower petals—seemingly in the name of pure peskiness.

One well-documented use of tools on a grand scale by crows around the world is the dropping of nuts on the road to be shelled by passing cars. The crows will swoop in, drop their nuts, and wait on a wire for a vehicle to pass. They will then swoop down again to see whether their nuts have been crushed open. Some scientists have dismissed these actions as unsubstantiated anecdote, but the incidents are now too widespread and well-observed to be taken lightly. In David Attenborough's 1998 documentary *The Life of Birds*, the crows in Tokyo were filmed taking this tack a step further. The streets were so busy with traffic, they couldn't fly in to inspect their flattened nuts without risking their lives. So they stood by the side of the road with the pedestrians waiting for the walk signal, and when it came on, they strode out with the other walkers to retrieve their nut meats. I have lived in West Seattle for more than a decade, and it is only in the last couple of years that I have seen crows regularly dropping nuts onto our busiest thoroughfare. I wonder, am I witnessing "morphic resonance," the biochemist Rupert Sheldrake's name for his theory that once an attitude, behavior, or action is "out there" in the world, it is picked up faster by other organisms? Have the crows all gathered in some secret corvid parlor to watch Attenborough's show? Or was I just not paying attention before? John Marzluff believes that an increase in nut dropping might simply be linked to an increase in nuts — if a nearby horse chestnut tree is yielding a bountiful harvest, we'll see more crows reaping it.

Meanwhile, down at Alki Beach the crows dislodge *Nucella* snails along the rocky shoreline, fly into the air, and drop them on the largest rocks, just as the gulls (another intelligent avian group) do with their recalcitrant shelled quarry. But if the snails do not break open, the crows, unlike gulls, will fly them over the road and wait for cars.

In a related crow story, one of the Alki crows collects the shells left after it eats the run-over snails. He carries them in his bill to a pile he keeps on the shrubby bank across the road, where he caches various treasures besides his snail shells—dried berries, foil gum wrappers, a piece of pink-and-silver zipper from a child's jacket. Collecting pretty things is a general habit of some bird species, such as the male bowerbirds of New Guinea and Australia; there are few reports of treasure-caching in the crow literature, though crow researchers acknowledge the many anecdotal reports of such behavior. I have watched this crow extensively, wondering what purpose his cache could possibly serve. Might he offer his treasures as "gifts" to a potential mate? If so, I haven't seen it. He will stand next to his cherished trove and rearrange it for several minutes. He seems to enjoy looking at it. He becomes agitated if another crow approaches, and even more annoyed if I try to sneak a closer look when he is anywhere near. Lately, I have been unable to find the cache, and I believe he may have moved it because of my intrusive curiosity, just as a mother cat will move her kittens if she thinks they are potentially in danger.

Some of the crow behaviors that seem so bewildering turn out to be well documented. On warm days, crows often take to sunning themselves, sitting still in the sunny grass, often sprawled on one side with their wings hanging open and their mandibles parted. They look like black-feathered Madame Bovarys, rapturously poisoned. Crows that are sunning appear drunk, a condition that is actually not uncommon in some birds. When robins eat berries that have begun to ferment in the late fall, like those of the mountain ash, they become tipsy and stupid. They will sit on back porches in drunken stupors, and we can sometimes walk right over and pick them up. Since crows are larger and sturdier than robins, such drunkenness is unlikely. A crow that appears drunk has probably sunken into the contemplative state that seems to fall on crows when they are sunning. This is one of the only times that crows relax their ready alertness.

In addition to their array of physical behaviors, crows share an extensive vocabulary, approaching a kind of language. Though the crow is officially a songbird, a member of the Passeriform order that includes the most gifted avian troubadors, such as the thrushes and warblers, few of us think of the crow's persistent "Caw! Caw! Caw!" as song. And unlike other songbirds, crows do not use their voices to attract a mate or vary their vocalizations much by season. There is no "dawn chorus" for crows; they vocalize all day and into the evening. As night falls on their massive evening roosts, they speak in crow whispers for a while before bursting again into full voice as the sun rises and they ascend from their branches — a raucous, exhilarating moment.

Though they don't sing, crows do vocalize wildly. Human attempts to construct a meaningful crow lexicon remain unsophisticated. "Our current knowledge is really only utilitarian," writes John Marzluff. "We know some basic words and phrases. It is as though we are traveling in a foreign country without speaking the language; we miss many cultural nuances. Until we can speak crow, we will not fully know the crow." *

We can't speak crow, but we have come to know some of the things they are "saying." In 1971, Dwight Chamberlain and George Cornwell published an oft-cited paper in the ornithological journal *The Auk,* in which they analyzed various crow calls they had recorded, and then measured the birds' responses to the calls when played back for them in various field contexts. The researchers were able to identify several vocalizations that the crows use to impart specific messages. Among them are the assembly call, the scolding call, the dispersal call, and the squalling call. This last is uttered by crows that are actually struggling to escape from a predator, such as a hawk. (The sound can be induced, the authors helpfully inform us, by "holding an immature or adult crow upside down by its legs and shaking it.") Chamberlain and Cornwell also catalog the moribund call, the threat call, the growl call, the immature hunger and feeding call, the contact call, the announcement call, duet notes, courtship vocalizations, and screams.

In all, the study documents twenty-three uniquely identifiable crow vocalizations, and the phrase "Crows are known to utilize 23 different vocalizations" is oft-repeated in

---

* Some might object to using the term *language* to refer to communication outside the human realm. Here I use the term somewhat colloquially to refer to a system of communication in use among a particular group. Corvid language is, of course, not nearly as involved as human language, but it is still highly complex—far beyond what ornithological science can yet confidently comprehend and certainly exceeding what most of us consider to be the communicative capacity of birds.

the literature. But it is important to note that Chamberlain and Cornwell say only that twenty-three vocalizations are described in this particular study. They are careful to point out that these are not nearly all of the crow sounds that are known either to themselves or to others.

Some current researchers suggest that it might be presumptuous to interpret the meaning of crow calls, and so label the various vocalizations descriptively rather than according to presumed function: the short caw, the medium caw, the harsh caw, the ko-aw, and on it goes. This is a respectful approach, but oftentimes we have to admit that the crow's message is perfectly clear.

In my Christmas stocking last year, I received a crow call. My mother had put it there, and she told me that she'd found it at a sporting goods store. I like to think of her there, waltzing past the rifles, the ammo, and the ferocious stuffed bear to inquire about a crow call for her vegetarian, bird-watching daughter. Crow calls are used not normally by bird-watchers but by crow hunters, who lure groups of crows in to shoot them. I was thrilled with my gift; I hadn't known there was such a thing. It takes a little practice to get a good crowish tone from the call, which is shaped like a squat kazoo and fitted with a plastic reed. My call, the packaging states, produces realistic sounds that make it "the choice of National Champions and weekend hunters alike." And it's true; it sounds pretty good. I carried it to Lincoln Park, an area of wooded trails leading to the Puget Sound shoreline near my home in Seattle, and a spot favored by many crows.

I tried the *assembly call* recommended in the crow call instructions, a two-part call with a smooth note followed by a raspy note. To my absolute surprise, the three crows that were already in the big-leaf maple over my head were joined, within thirty seconds, by a *dozen* more. This was just a very few of the crows in the entire park, but it was an impressive result, I thought, for the crow call debut. No matter what could be said about the difficulty of learning crow language, clearly the assembly call, even when attempted on a kazoo that made it sound to me very much like a duck, means "Assemble!" I thought about attempting to learn other crow vocalizations with my little crow kazoo, but truly, it is not good birder ethics to overuse vocalizations; it messes with the heads of the birds you are attempting to observe and perhaps with those of many others. With a new respect for its potential power, I happily dropped the crow call in my top desk drawer.

I did, however, redouble my efforts to discern meaning in crow vocalizations. Several calls are described time and again in my notebooks, and without thinking much about it, I attached my own homespun names to them. When most of us think of crow language, we think of the *typical caw* that is often made when birds come in for landing. It appears to be a kind of announcement: "I am here if anybody cares, and even if they don't." This caw carries some distance, and birds in flight use a version of it to stay in contact with one another. This also seems to be the default crow caw, used when they have nothing in particular to communicate, but feel like cawing anyway, or as a form of displacement behavior when they are nervous and don't know what else to do. Sometimes such caws are structured (given in bursts of two or more caws of equal duration), and sometimes unstructured (given at seemingly random intervals). They may be accompanied by head bobbing and tail spreading. It is likely that even though these caws may seem to us to serve no particular purpose, they are fraught with meaning to the crows who give or receive them.

Crows do not reserve their vocal discourse for one another; sometimes they talk directly to us. The best-known crow-to-human communication is probably the *remonstration call*, familiar to anyone who has ventured too close to a crow's nest or young. It is very similar to the *chick in the wrong place call*, oft heard in late spring, and it involves a long, threatening, screechy holler at the offending subject. I do want to be careful about assigning particular translations to crow language, but these birds are not mincing words. This call plainly means, "You there! Vile creature! Move along this minute!" Perhaps also, "Or else!" These calls will follow you until you achieve a prescribed distance known only to the crow, though the bird will usually keep an eye on you for a bit longer than its vocal scolding lasts. The remonstration is rarely given without reason, so if you are its victim, be sure to take a moment to see what the fuss is about. The crow-family dynamics are fascinating to observe, and the intensity of the bird's reprimand will mount and fade as you tread closer or farther away. Be careful to gauge the crow's level of parental zeal; during certain seasons you could be dive-bombed.

My favorite crow vocalization is what I call *pillow talk*. At the nest in the evening, and especially at the evening roosts during the nonbreeding seasons, crows talk in hushed, sleepy, murmuring whispers. This sometimes accompanies a putting together of heads and allopreening. These are also the first vocalizations of the morning, before the day gets going and caws come into full swing. It's calming and lovely.

Crows are capable mimics, and mimicry is a category of crow vocalization unto itself. Theories abound, but no one is certain whether it has some purpose beyond play or self-amusement. Steller's Jays, corvid relatives of the crow, will often mimic Red-tailed Hawks near a bird feeder in an effort to scare off smaller songbirds, and get the seed for themselves. Crows don't seem to use mimicry this way—nor do they need to. They are big enough to frighten away smaller birds on their own. Chamberlain and Cornwell suggest that mimicry serves to strengthen individual pair bonds; a bird may learn the specific vocal tendencies of its mate, and they may repeat unique phrases to each other as a means of maintaining contact and perhaps closeness. Chamberlain studied eight tame crows and attested to the fact that in captivity, crows learn to imitate the human voice. His favorite in this category was an adult male crow in West Virginia who could say quite clearly, "Oh my God! Oh Lord!" Crows are also known to mimic Barred Owls, crying children, cats, dogs, ducks, geese, and roosters.

Perhaps the most instructive category of crow vocalization is the large one labeled *Other*. Crows sometimes coo, whisper, whine, meow, croak, chuckle, whinny, and presumably make all sorts of other sounds that I have never heard. No matter how earnestly we study, it is likely we will never comprehend the full range and meaning of crow language.

Throughout much of the crow-year, vocal communication is reinforced by physical closeness. During the courtship and breeding season, birds pair up and fan out, nesting somewhat territorially. But in the autumn, the birds begin to gather again in great roosting aggregations, often returning to the same place year after year in astonishing numbers — hundreds, thousands, tens of thousands, sometimes even more. Two million crows have been counted at a roost site in Oklahoma.

This roosting behavior is not uncommon in the bird world, and certainly not limited to crows, but because crows are so large and loud, their roosts seem particularly spectacular and ominous. Crows roost communally for various reasons, the foremost probably being protection. In a group of thousands of birds, the chance that you are going to be the one picked up for dinner by the Peregrine Falcon is slim. But crows also gather for social reasons. Adult birds find mates, young birds learn new vocalizations and postures and how to behave like a good crow. It is possible that roosting crows share information about food sources at their evening congregations (as ravens are known to do). In the morning, crows begin to wake up and whisper together, and the conversations soon turn to cacophony as thousands of birds spring into their day.

. . .

All of these activities and vocalizations speak to crows' extraordinary intelligence and to the remarkable plasticity of their behavior. Not rigidly bound by instinct, crows can, and will, do just about anything. Much of what we see crows do is covered in the ornithological literature. Much is not and never will be.

Once I saw a crow sitting on a wire as a gentle breeze loosed a cloud of cherry blossom petals. She tried, like a playful cat, to catch the petals one at a time with her bill as they drifted by. Once after a rare Seattle snow, I saw two crows standing up to their bellies in snowfall. They gathered the snow on their heads and tossed it up, then jumped after it with their bills as it fell around them, enjoying the novelty in very much the same manner as Claire and I were. Once I saw a crow climbing the ladder my neighbor had left against his cherry tree. It started at the bottom rung, jumped to the next, and the next, until it reached the top, then flew to the bottom and started over. These stories might not be suitable for a scientific journal, but they are fitting for our own field notebooks, for our naturalist's diaries, for the tales we tell, and for the private places where we keep and treasure our own observations of the wild earth's wonders, whether they occur thousands of times over or are written only once.

Every day, crows offer a manageable peek into the difficult complexity of the natural world. But the more I watch them, the more their stories speak two messages: the seen and the unseen. Even when their physical bodies are not telling tales in front of me, I find they have left little missives strewn about, "pages" lined with nests, pellets, half-eaten cherries, droppings, tracks, and feathers. The crow's vivid scrawl does more than inform me about crows; it reminds me of the other wild creatures that ceaselessly encircle me, writing stories of their own unseen lives, leaving their own scripted clues, more quietly perhaps, more lightly, but just as truly.

One morning I was sitting at my desk writing before anyone else was up. I looked out to see a crow on top of the utility pole in front of our house, with an oddly shaped something beneath its feet. I lifted my binoculars and couldn't believe my eyes. That crow had a bat! He was trying to eat the bat but was clearly unnerved by the process. The elastic patagia of the bat's wings were unruly and kept snapping out from under the crow's feet. As soon as one part of the bat was under control, another part would escape, flapping askew. The bird kept shaking his head and wiping his bill, as if the bat were unsettlingly sticky. I smiled. Here was one dark, misunderstood animal eating another. But then I scowled. I am a bat lover. One of the first things I did in order to begin the reconciliation of my urban-wild house with my still unstable mind was to install a bat box beneath the east-facing eaves. (The empty cavities of decaying trees are increasingly scarce in urban places, and bat houses can help restore the balance.) Every evening, I kept my eye on the bat box's egress. I scanned the dusken sky for signs of their small, erratic flight. And I had begun to conclude, reluctantly, that there must be no bats in our new neighborhood. Now this. Not only could I plainly see that there were bats among us after all, but I was reminded afresh of one of the crow's most contradictory purposes in my biological education: *in their bold visibility, crows show me what I don't see.*

After the crow flew away (messy-billed and bat in tow), I tiptoed out on the dewy grass to see whether there were any bits of bat left beneath the pole. I found a few tiny fluffs of gray-brown fur, soft as a chinchilla's. Had I not seen the crow with the bat, I am sure I would never have noticed these tiny bat clues.

Aldo Leopold believed that our missteps regarding the natural world very often arise from a lack of "ecological perception," from our "inability to read the land." For Leopold, land is more a concept than a place, expansively involving "all things on, over, or in the earth." He taught that the stories told by these various dimensions of the land are something we can learn to interpret, a narrative text that we can read. In my understanding of Leopold, he was not speaking by way of analogy; his "reading" implies the literal presence of a kind of writing, an epistle as sure as any penned by human hands. The narrative Leopold speaks of is an intricate one, unfolding beneath our everyday awareness. In the past, humans have written the stories of wild animals in our own stilted text, and though we have at times been thoughtful scribes, we have just as often misconstrued the land's meaning and let our misconstructions stand in our science, our politics, and our cultural mythology. But the wild beings have their own stories to tell, and in the reading of their singular alphabet—their tracks, voices, homes, scat, feathers, presence, and absence—we may find that they sometimes object to things we have always believed to be true.

Attempting to read crow lives attunes my eyes to this quieter, penciled world—its stories, its struggles, its needs. It inspires me to watch for the next layer, and then the next. In our urban watching, we learn to remain alert to the presence of the wild on earth, to grow an awareness that is an essential counterbalance to the isolating loss of wild knowledge that urban and suburban living so typically brings.

We heard the Indigo Girls play an outdoor concert at the zoo last summer. It was the end of the season, and the crows were beginning to gather in the numbers that would characterize their great autumn flocks, swirling in the dusk. There were enough of them to make people start looking skyward, pointing, and to make those with the common, subrational crow fear start feeling edgy. A few songs into the first set, about twenty crows settled in a tree at the edge of the field, and every one of them sat there quietly, with toes and faces pointed toward the stage. Were they enjoying the music? At the break, the crows flew off, but they returned when the Girls came back onstage and started the second set. I watched the three on the "front-row" branch. Were they—? I can hardly suggest it, and it was barely perceptible. *Were they nodding their heads in time?* "If the world is night—shine my life like a light."

Four

WALKING

The Wildness of Home

Choose your instrument asking only: can you play it while walking?

— JAY GRIFFITHS

Like many of us, I read Henry David Thoreau's famous manifesto *Walking* when I was in college, and it reaffirmed the feelings I had experienced after reading it in high school. "Yes," I whispered, my fervent young idealism nearly at a pitch with the Concordian pencil maker's, *"I am in love with him."* Never mind that *Walking* devolved at its center into a patriotic ode to manifest destiny. Like most budding eco-philosophers who took Thoreau as their doyen, I chose to ignore that bit. Instead, I lolled in the grass beneath the trees, just where I knew Thoreau would want me, the book over my face. "I wish to make an extreme statement," he brashly declared. I wish to "speak a word for Nature," to "regard man as an inhabitant, or a part and parcel of Nature." Yes! And the way into such glorious part-and-parcel-ness? The wildness of walking. No mere taking of air or exercise, this walking, no simple swinging of dumbbells or strapping on of pedometers so that we know we have reached our allotted five thousand steps and can now go back home. No. This walking was "in itself the enterprise and adventure of the day." And better still, "Every walk is a sort of crusade," in which we "go forth and reconquer this Holy Land from the hands of the Infidels." How ardent his voice! How worthy, ravishing, and true! And so I walked everywhere. I walked *barefoot*, moreover, the mile from my apartment to campus and back several times every day. Though I have read that our skin cells are replaced every thirty-five days, my heels have never revived and are permanently cracked and callused, like a cloven-hoofed beast's.

What I am about to say will come as no surprise whatsoever. For the self-styled urban naturalist, walking is an essential way of getting about, at least part of the time. Cycling and riding buses are wonderful ways to build community, reduce our ecological impact, and "save the earth." But if we want also to *know* the earth, to cultivate reverence, to look to wild nature in its myriad forms for inspiration, mentoring, sustenance, and perhaps correction, then walking is a necessary practice.

Clearly this is not an original thought. It has been said innumerable times across the millennia, in countless ways and by varied thinkers. Nearly twenty-four hundred years ago in ancient Greece, Aristotle led a school of peripatetic philosophers who understood that bodily movement increased the breadth of their thought, and who constructed leafy outdoor malls through which to stroll and ruminate. Before them, Plato told a story about his student the philosopher-mathematician Thales, who preferred to think while ambulating and famously walked right into a ditch while contemplating the night sky. "How do you expect to understand what is going on up in the sky if you do not even see what is at your feet?" queried the servant girl who rushed to help him, clearly knowing a thing or two about walking herself.

We have been told that walking is a way into our own intelligence and creativity. It is commonplace for modern writers to agree with Thoreau, who claimed to write best, both in terms of quality and quantity, in direct proportion to how much he walked. In *If You Want to Write*, the book first published in 1938 that continues to mentor so many writers across genres, Barbara Ueland recommends walking as a way into the thoughts we don't even know we have: "If when I walk I look at the sky or the lake or the tiny, infinitesimally delicate, bare, young trees, or wherever I want to look, and my neck and jaw are loose and I feel happy and say to myself with my imagination, 'I am free,' and 'There is nothing to hurry about,' I find then that thoughts begin to come to me in their quiet way." (Her book's subtitle is telling: *A Book About Art, Independence, and Spirit.*)

Walker-thinkers have found various ways to accommodate the gifts of imagination that their walking brings. Caught paperless on his walks in the Czech enclaves of Iowa, maestro Dvořák scribbled the string quartets that visited his brain on his starched white shirt cuffs (so the legend goes). More proactively, Thomas Hobbes fashioned a walking stick for himself with an inkwell attached, and modern poet Mary Oliver leaves pencils in the trees along her usual pathways, in case a poem descends during her rambles. In England we have Wordsworth, Coleridge, Tennyson, Keats, Mary Wollstonecraft, and Matthew Arnold, among others, peopling a romantic "Walkers' Hall of Fame." In America, famous ramblers in our twined natural and literary history include Audubon, Thoreau, his sometimes-friend Emerson, and Walt Whitman. The journals of Meriwether Lewis, served by his walking nearly one thousand miles, are filled with the detailed natural history observations that can be gathered only on foot. More recently Rebecca Solnit, seeking a way into her book of essays on walking, began with a walk: "My circuit was almost finished, and at the end of it I knew what my subject was and how to address it in a way I had not six miles before."

Walking is the pace that we were born to. It is the pace at which our eyes can focus, our thoughts can keep up, and our bodies can feel evolved and grounded and whole. Walking, we are on an axis about which we can turn to look, or bend to see, or squat to pick up. Walking, we feel knowing and self-reliant, inhabitants of our own bodies, and in cahoots with the bodies of others.

Thoreau is interested in the *manner* of walking. Unfolding his sense of wild walking as an art, he launches into a fascinating false etymology:

> I have met with but one or two persons in the course of my life who understood the art of Walking, that is, of taking walks—who had a genius, so to speak, for *sauntering*, which word is beautifully derived "from idle people who roved about the country, in the Middle Ages, and asked charity, under pretense of going "*a la Sainte Terre*," to the Holy Land, till the children

exclaimed, "There goes a *Sainte-Terrer,*" a Saunterer, a Holy-Lander.

He goes on, mining yet another etymological fiction, to say that *saunter* might derive instead from *sans terre,* "without a land or a home," which Thoreau spins positively as being "equally at home everywhere."* This, he proclaims, is the secret of successful sauntering, and his point is well made, foggy etymology notwithstanding. The whole essay, I think, turns upon one gorgeously rabid point, where Thoreau tells us just what ought to be at stake in our walking: "We should go forth on the shortest walk, perchance, in the spirit of undying adventure, never to return,—prepared to send back our embalmed hearts only as relics to our desolate kingdoms."

I remember well my youthful "yes" to this very paragraph. My *embalmed heart in a box!* The reference is to the Crusades; when nobles were felled and their bodies could not be lugged home, their hearts were embalmed and delivered to loved ones for burial. How glorious this artful, wild sauntering! With my beloved Henry David, I would settle

---

* It appears that Thoreau was taking Samuel Johnson's 1755 *Dictionary of the English Language* as his source. The modern lexicographic scholarship states that the origin of *saunter* is unknown, though Eric Partridge ventures the Middle French possibility *s'aunter,* "to advance oneself," to move forward, perhaps from the older French *avant,* "to be in front of, or in advance of." *Merriam-Webster* suggests a link to the Middle English *santren,* "to muse." In any case, the poetic sensibility we love in sauntering, with its willowlike movement, emerged in the seventeenth century, but without the overlay of romantic history imparted by Thoreau, Johnson, and others both before and after them.

for no less. They could embalm both our hearts and bury them together! Now I look at this very same paragraph and I laugh. Not derisively, and not even because I have changed my mind, on the whole. I still feel that regular walking is, in this country, one of the most essential and effective eco-revolutionary measures that we can all take. But still. There will be no embalming of hearts today, thank you very much. "I have lost the idealism of my twenties, as I feared I would," wrote Annie Dillard. Yes, but there is more to it than that. I realize that in giving birth, managing a household, raising a child, and composting potato peels in a city, I have learned some things about wildness that even Thoreau could not have known.

Besides humans and pigeons, crows are the most common city and suburban walkers. I am quite sure that their affinity for terrestrial existence is one of the facts of crow life that has made humans over time take such notice of them; the combination of their bipedalism (or semi-bipedalism, for of course they can fly as well) and intelligence forces us to look at crows with a kind of recognition. We pay our best attention to animals that lie within our general geographical sphere, that is, between the sidewalk and about nine or ten feet up. Beyond that—too far above or too far below—our ability to easily identify a creature fails or takes too much effort. Our interest, and perhaps our courage, falters. But crows hang out right here with us, not just on the earth, but on the disturbed earth, on the sidewalks where we take our own exercise. And unlike other animals who walk on our sidewalks with our blessing (our dogs and cats) and those that walk on our sidewalks without our blessing, or usually even our knowledge (nocturnal raccoons, possums, and rats), crows are bipedal. Like us.

Many of the species in various avian families and orders walk: pigeons, pheasants, gulls, ducks, shorebirds, ostriches, and others. But the large Passeriform order, to which the corvid family belongs, is not known for walking. The evolutionary radiation of passerines was arboreal—they adapted to life in the trees and proliferated there. Though they are often called songbirds, *perching birds* is the more accurate colloquialism. Passerines share several physiological characteristics, but the most constant is in the construction of their feet and legs. They have three toes pointing forward and one to the rear, and curved, pointed nails—all for strong perching and gripping—as well as involuntary leg muscles that help them grasp their branch and not fall off when distracted or sleeping. The great majority of passerines rarely, if ever, spend time on the ground, and when they do, they will not walk at all—they are not able. They hop.

There are exceptions, and some familiar passerines are excellent walkers. Robins and the rest of the thrushes, starlings, pipits, and others all walk one foot at a time, and some of them even run. This is an indication that it has been some time in their evolutionary history since they descended from their arboreal passerine past to reap the benefits of foraging on terra firma. Their muscles have adapted, over time, to walking. All corvids walk, and among them, crows are typically the most terrestrial of all.

On land, crows prefer to walk, though they often hop. I have spent hours watching crows decide whether to walk or to hop, and in general it appears that they hop when they get nervous and want to move quickly away from the source of anxiety, or when they suddenly feel like they want to get somewhere in a hurry but can't quite be bothered to fly. Though moving quickly seems to be their objective, it is not at all clear that hopping crows actually move much faster than walking crows. The hopping, not a two-footed jump but more of a sideways-skipping sashay, is rather inefficient. I tried to measure the relative speed of the two modes by putting small wooden posts in a wide grassy space at Lincoln Park where crows gather in numbers, thinking I might catch crows walking or hopping between them, time them, and get some sense of how fast they move from one place to another in each gait. I should have known that was a ridiculous idea. Once they got over the horror of little sticks in their yard (crows are unnerved by novelty), they absolutely refused to walk anywhere near them, much less from one to the other. So my impression that hopping is not faster than walking is purely subjective, though I can say with some certainty that if it is faster, it is not *much* faster.

If we picked up a crow, most of us would be surprised at how light and delicate it would feel. Crows are small under all those feathers, with hollow bones for lightness in flight. They weigh almost nothing. Their legs would seem particularly insubstantial. We could easily snap the brittle tibiotarsus between our fingers. It is a slender, sharp bone, pointed along the front ridge, like our own tibia. The feet would seem small and flexible, hardly suited to their rugged life. Yet for a passerine bird, crows have substantial feet. The toes are somewhat flared with exaggerated padding, and they are roughly scaled at the ends, and smoother toward the center. Their feet are the same color, perhaps a tad lighter, than the plumage covering the bird. Crow toenails are dark gray, thick for a perching bird, pointed, and somewhat curved. The feet tell the story of a bird whose life reaches from soil to tree and beyond, all in equal measure. The names of the bones are the same as those in our own feet and legs. There are tarsals, metatarsals, tibia, and femur. There are toes, an ankle, a knee, a hip.

Many people think that birds have backward-bending knees, like the hind legs of a horse. But in fact birds walk on their toes, with an elongated "shin" leading to a back-crooked ankle. The tibiotarsus leads from this joint to an actual knee, usually hidden close to the bird's body and covered with feathers, and a thick femur then connects to the pelvis.

Crows are pigeon-toed, much more so than actual pigeons, which is why they waddle so much when they walk. If you watch just about any other walking bird, whether it is a passerine or not—a robin, say, or a gull—and imagine that its feet are making tracks, you will see that the tracks would run in two parallel lines. But crows often step one foot in front of the other, as if attempting to walk the line on a DUI test, forcing their tails to waggle to and fro behind them.

Humans have evolved more specific adaptations for bipedalism than crows, but it is only in recent geological time that hominid primates have become fully bipedal, and some compromises were wrung in the evolutionary deal. Our closest living relatives, the chimpanzees, walk on two feet now and then and for short distances, but usually they knuckle-walk. They cannot fully extend their knees or lock their legs straight, as humans can. When chimps stand or walk upright, they have to work their leg muscles to hold themselves up, which is tiring. In humans, the femur, or thigh-bone, angles inward from the hip to the knee, resulting in feet placed neatly under our center of gravity. When we walk, the well-honed gluteal abductors to the side of the hip contract and keep us from tipping sideways while one of our feet bears our full weight in midstride. Our spine has evolved a double curve, unique among vertebrates, that allows our head and torso to line up vertically above our feet. But the arrangement is not perfect. We walk with ease, but our skeleton is not particularly stable. Atheists point to the human knee as an argument against the existence of God (an intelligent designer would never have allowed such an atrocity), and we are subject to frequent spinal strain, injury, and disc compression. In modern quadrupeds we can see how spines functioned before the advent of hominid bipedalism — like a "flexible suspension bridge," the biology teachers say, supporting the various organs and not subject to the pressure of a fully upright posture.

Foraging crows, if they don't feel threatened, will walk for hours in fields or at park edges or on the beach. On Puget Sound, near our home, I watch them for as long as they'll stay. Absorbed in their walking, making notes and sketches, observing their gait and waddle, concocting ill-fated experiments, I almost forget sometimes that they can fly and am startled out of my reverie by the sudden easy flap and lift. I feel the weight of my body, heavier than I'd remembered. But in a block's walk, I am light again. Immersed in the prevailing artificiality of consumer culture, we forget the earthen capabilities of our bodies, where they can take us, and how far. But how easy it is to remember, and remember again.

Thoreauvian walkers know where we like to walk best. We like to walk in Nature. Capital N nature. With trees tinkling shadowy over our heads, and the thunk of a wood-rot pathway guiding our feet, with grasses brushing our thighs, or a stony escarpment sweeping up our side. We shamelessly proclaim our romantic aspirations. We want to feel renewal in stillness and birdsong and the hidden movement of worms, the unabashed truth of decay. We want to pay attention, to know the wonders of life in secret places, to watch and be watched, to learn and unlearn.

Ready for my daily walk, I tie on my Keen Urbanator sneakers and step onto the porch. (Would I have bought them even without the resonant suggestion of the brilliant young catalog copywriter who proclaimed these to be the ideal shoes for bravely slogging the "urban jungle"? Probably. But I decided that while I was about it, I would fully enjoy the marketing imagery.) And always, though I feel ready for any eventuality, it is pretty much as I expected. Three crows on a wire suspended over a concrete sidewalk. Not a wood-rot path in sight. Many a tree, the native firs and cedars crowded by surrounding ornamentals. And of course I don't even bother about an escarpment. There is, instead, a stripey pattern as far as I can see: asphalt street, bordered by a stripe of grass, then a stripe of sidewalk, then another stripe of grass, then a house. The pattern is stippled with "street trees," species approved by the city. They are Korean dogwood, hawthorn, purple-leaved thundercloud plums, or, like ours, forest redbud pansies—beautiful trees, but not a native in the bunch. And of course the whole is outlined with assorted garden botanicals, many of them very pretty, some tidy, some sprawling.

Our feet, I am sure, can tell the difference between the substance of nature and the artifice of human construct. This is one of the reasons that bare feet love and seek sand, mud, warm, worn stone, grasses, soil, tidal flats, the shallow, rocky edges of lakes. This is why we feel a frisson of recognition and unexpected joy when we allow our feet their rare forays into outdoor shoelessness. "You should make her wear sandals," a mother tells me, watching our daughters at the beach. "Sometimes there's glass." I look around for glassy edges, then at Claire's loose, free feet, clouded in sand. I nod at my friend, who is, of course, right. "She'll be fine," I tell her.

As an apprentice urban nature walker, I keep stumbling over sidewalks, wondering over the role of such artifice when what I really want is to be a modern Charlotte Brontë, wandering the windswept moors. Sidewalks are made of concrete, and two very different constituencies make the bumper-sticker claim that "Concrete Is Forever!" Eco-activists, opposing the spread of more despoiling, earth-covering, erosion-causing, flood-inducing concrete parking lots, roads, and sidewalks (not to mention dams), point to concrete's impervious permanence, alongside its sheer ubiquity, as its primary evil. (I read that concrete is the most commonly used human-made material on earth. By 2005, there were six billion cubic meters of concrete poured *every year*—that's roughly one for every person on the planet.) Concrete companies, ready to pour us new versions of all of the above, point to concrete's nonporous permanence as its primary virtue. Both sides are right—concrete is hard and tough and difficult to get rid of (hence a thing is said to be "set in concrete" when it is perceived as fixed and unalterable). But both are also wrong—concrete is far from permanent, especially as a

sidewalk. Concrete sidewalks crack. They crack as they settle, as they weather, and as they are contorted by the roots
of growing trees. These cracks fill with ants, soil, seeds, and
eventually plants, whose roots invade and split the concrete
further. Water enters and plays at the semiporous edges,
then freezes, expanding to create even more cracks. Sidewalks are poured by humans, and as such are subject to the
usual human miscalculations and errors, especially those that
surface when we fail to properly gauge the interplay of our
own designs with the forces of wild nature. Over geological time, concrete will normally degrade faster than much
naturally occurring stone. This is small comfort as we see
the earth paved over beneath our very noses. Still, it is something, and I am ready to grasp at any straw in my path.

For the urban nature walker with little choice, sidewalks
require our attention. Surely we can't just sit on our wid-
ening bums, bemoaning the distance to a proper woodland
path. Sidewalks are, after all, a kind of path themselves, and
the obvious point of departure for a walk in our home ecosystem. They might be made of concrete, but they are also a
force of imagination. They exist as testament to the human
intent and desire to walk, a symbol of our shared sense of
the value and necessity of traveling *a pied,* and of the creating and sustaining a means to do so. There is inspiration
here and the potential for adventure and — does it sound too
silly to say? — even a kind of danger.

Okay, yes, it sounds silly, but do consider: How many
times have you tripped on a sidewalk? How many times
have you seen people walking innocently down a sidewalk,

expecting it to be flat and supporting, only to trip where it unexpectedly buckles, as crooked as a talus trail? In Seattle, there are countless complaints to the city about dangerous sidewalks and even, in recent years, two wrongful death lawsuits. In the majority of dangerous-sidewalk cases, roots are to blame, pushing through the seeming permanence with the unstoppable tenacity of growth. The revenge of the trees.

My purpose is not to romanticize sidewalks—I remain firmly planted in the "Stumps Suck" and the "Concrete Is Forever" camp of eco-activism. Still, I do want to see sidewalks for what they are. Concretions of sand, minerals, stony aggregate, and water. They are made of earth, subject to the forces of nature, and today, for most of us, they are both footpath and invitation, beckoning us out of the house and off the road, into the surprising interplay of our bodies with the landscape surrounding our homes.

And certainly the sidewalk is not the end in itself unless we allow it to be. It leads as far as we would like, and in the direction we choose. While cars are strapped to their little tracks, we on the sidewalks traverse edges lightly, stepping over concrete margins onto grasses, soil, stone. Sidewalks take us through and to everything that is not a sidewalk. And all sidewalks lead, eventually, to their own end. In the question of *how to live,* sidewalks are a reminder of where we want to be headed, for surely we cannot declare that we are "off the beaten path" if we aren't, at least at first, on it.

Nevertheless, I realize that for Thoreau, this sidewalk-lined tangle of human habitations is exactly what we are called to walk away from. As urban dwellers go, I am fortunate in that I can do that, at least somewhat. If I walk ten minutes to the west, toward the water, I will be in the middle of Lincoln Park, one of Seattle's largest and most beautiful refuges, a 137-acre preserve of trails, native trees and plants, resident and migrant birds, and a stretch of Puget Sound shoreline that brings, in winter, seabirds that we would normally have to travel to the coast to see—murres, auklets, and Pacific Loons. It wouldn't be enough for Thoreau, but for a forest-craving city girl, this is sanctuary indeed. I walk there most days, botanizing, crow-studying, bird-watching, daydreaming. I realize that in this I am blessed. For most people, urban and suburban, such natural sustenance is harder won, if walking to a place that could colloquially pass as nature is possible at all. But for my current project of more fully understanding my home ecosystem, I finally had to admit that Lincoln Park was too easy. Of course I could find natural refuge there. In a gorgeous, forested park surrounded by shoreline and the glacier-carved Olympic Mountains range, who couldn't? But Lincoln Park is just the green-ruffled edge of my neighborhood. I want to dig deeper, edgier, rougher. Where is the tenacious wild, and how do I come to find it, see it, know it? How do I come under its influence? And—especially—how do I help it to flourish?

Lincoln Park and its birds and trees are ten minutes west, by foot. If I walk twenty minutes southeast, I am someplace else altogether, in Westwood Village, a shopping complex anchored by big boxes such as Target, Staples, and Barnes & Noble, and strung together with smaller chain stores—RadioShack, Pier One, Jamba Juice, and of course Starbucks (*two* of them)—and, surprisingly, a couple of locally owned restaurants, including Vatsana's Thai Restaurant, where the proprietor is herself from Thailand and comes in every day to oversee the making of the sauces. Unlike the park crows, who complement picnic fare with tideland invertebrates, the shopping center crows are concrete specialists, tearing at bags of McDonald's fries, Target popcorn, and discarded pizza crusts much of the day. By rights it seems they should look scrappy and thin, but they do not. I have often thought these are the fattest, shiniest, most handsome crows that I have ever seen.

Today I have a shopping list: scrubbing sponges, a bag of clothespins, envelopes, toothpaste, and a new box of crayons for Claire, as I inadvertently left hers in a sunny window and they melted into a colorful mess. Now, of course, I must officially go on record as detesting the big boxes, and for all the usual reasons that thinking people already know and share. Even so, there is just one place within walking distance that will have all of these things, reasonably priced. No matter how I stack it, this is a job for Target. So I tie on my Urbanators, don my fashionable binoculars, and set off, intent upon crossing items off one list while creating another.

Birds Seen Between Our House and Target

European Starling
American Goldfinch
Bewick's Wren

Violet-green Swallow
Barn Swallow
Anna's Hummingbird
American Crow
American Robin
Bushtit
House Sparrow
White-crowned Sparrow
Rock Dove (pigeon)
Steller's Jay
Cedar Waxwing
Black-capped Chickadee

Of these, only three—the European Starling, House Sparrow, and Rock Dove—do not really belong; that is, they are non-native. Two of these, the swallows, are neotropical migrants, flying all the way to Seattle each spring from Mexico or Central or South America. The others are native residents, living and nesting here, as I do.

This list is unremarkable. These are exactly the birds I would expect to see today, in this season and in this place. But in just that short a walk, and in the city, how often do I really bother to see them? I consider the error of my ways, somehow allowing these birds to count less in my life, not quite meeting the criteria for a *wonder of nature,* even from my impoverished vantage of a city sidewalk. But of course they *do* count. Here, on the road to Target, these birds are as insistent as any secretive forest thrush upon their own wild necessity.

Continuing my walk, I crane my neck for more; but no, that is all. In a less disturbed habitat, the numbers would be greater, and the surprises—in the form of species I had not remembered to expect—would be more numerous. I feel that absence keenly. The watered-down homogeneity, the diminished diversity, the absolute loss of the most sensitive species. True intimacy with the places that we live implies this intimation of what is missing, and includes a sense of what might be recovered along with what is heartbreakingly lost. With conflicted gratitude, I look again at my bird list, what is given, for now, for today, in this place. I want to keep walking; perhaps there will be one more bird species, after all. But glancing at my watch I realize I have to rush back—my daughter is returning from school, and I have to be home.

Thoreau might have understood this impulse to turn homeward. He writes as if he were daily walking to the edge of cliffs and falling off them, but his boldest, most rebellious statement on walking really has nothing to do with embalmed body parts. It has to do with a sweet, spare household around which he tended a small patch of beans, returning daily to thin the seedlings, water them, and eventually eat them. Thoreau's central parable was the human creation of the earthly holt, the home that might resist prevailing tendencies and make some kind of sense.

Whenever I set out on an evening walk, it is with the intent of being home by bedtime. Home, where the wild things are. Home, where my flush-faced progeny waits for me to read *Charlotte's Web* before she slips into one more night's dreaming. Home, where the other animals have gone too at the end of their day's walking. To the roost, the hollow, the curl in the meadow. We feel the imperative, both in our biology and in our spirit. After a certain distance, a certain passing of time well walked (different for each person, and changing with the circumstances of the day), the sense comes to us. The walk has ended; the pull of the hearth is true. And though part of us longs to walk with Thoreau until our feet are bloody and moss settles into our tresses, the call is, also, sweet. Look up at dusk. The crows are flying to their great evening roosts. We follow them home.

Five

DWELLING

How We Nest

Wherefore when boughs are free —
Households in every tree —
Pilgrim be found?

— EMILY DICKINSON

My friends' moms don't do this," Claire reports skeptically as I hang the family skivvies on a clothesline with wooden pins that belonged to my mother. I have had to rig up a retractable line between the back porch and the cherry tree at the far end of the yard because Tom refused to sanction the building of a more permanent clothesline. It would take up half the yard, he claimed, and there are about three days a year that it doesn't rain. It's true: Seattle is not known for its clotheslines. But my solution works well enough and holds a full load of clothes if I am judicious about spacing. I pontificate to Claire about energy, water, the earth. Here in the Northwest our electricity comes mainly from hydropower rather than coal, so instead of talking about global warming, I remind her about dams and salmon. Claire points out that I am the only person she knows on the planet who is doing this, so it cannot possibly make any difference. To my surprise, she becomes visibly agitated. I cannot tell what upsets her more—the fact that more people don't dig out the clothespins or the spectacle of her beloved mother engaged in an act of utter futility. She formulates the well-worn question for herself: "What difference does it make if just one person does something?"

I sigh and stand up straight. "Look, sweetie…" I point and we watch one of the crows that has been building a nest in the neighbor's Douglas fir fly over with yet another stick. His mate is waiting there, takes the stick and places it herself (one of these birds has an albinistic patch on its wing, and I was fortunate enough to see this pair copulate, white-patch bird on top, so I know who is who). We have been watching their progress from certain well-chosen, neck-craning spots in our own yard. This is one of the three neighborhood nests we are monitoring, and we guess which flying crow-sticks are destined for which nests by the direction the crows are headed. It is spring. Good for nabbing the few dry Seattle days to hang laundry out to dry, and even better for watching the wonders of crow nesting and breeding unfold, as they do each year. The nests, now, are taking shape.

Crow nests look coarse and prickly from the outside, built as they are from a mingling of sticks. Crows take a great deal of time choosing the sticks they want to use in the construction of their nests. Often they use twigs that they find on the ground, but most crows break fresh twigs off trees as well. I have watched crows work in earnest, and at length, sometimes taking more than twenty minutes to disconnect one small twig from its larger branch. They brace their feet and pull forcefully with their bill, swinging their heads vigorously to loosen the chosen switch. They change tack, peck at the twig's base to loosen its connection, then pull again. Sometimes they give up for a while but come back again later. *"What,"* I want to shout out my window, "could possibly be so great about *that* stick?" There are a dozen like it on the ground. Of course fresh sticks are less brittle, and they can be bent nicely into nest shape, but it really does hardly seem worth all the work. I have also seen crows borrow sticks from nests of previous years—either their own, or others'—and occasionally purloin sticks from the nest that another pair is building, watching for them to leave, then swooping in to abscond with a choice twig.

A crow pair chooses a site and builds its nest together, usually in the upper third of a medium-size tree. Curiously, rural crows regularly build lower in their trees than urban crows do, perhaps because of the urban proximity to busy sidewalks (and hence, dogs, children, skateboards, and any number of other things that make crows nervous). In fact, it appears that crows are as ambivalent as I am about raising offspring in a city. Led by John Marzluff, researchers at the University of Washington studying crow demographics in the Seattle area have found that winter crow numbers are much higher than expected given the number of breeding birds in the area—that is, there are not enough nesters in the spring to account for all the crows here in the winter. It appears that while many Seattle crows live the urban life for a few years—being social and fattening up on urban delicacies like rats and french fries—they often leave the city at breeding age to nest and raise their young in the suburbs, where the air is cleaner, the streets are wider, the territories are broader, the trees are more numerous, and there is a lot of nice nutritious road kill (more possums, squirrels, and raccoons, maybe, and fewer rats). Some of the young from these nests head back to the city to spend their feckless youth, driving up winter crow numbers. Seattle's crow demographics are not known to be universal, and studies need to be undertaken in other urban areas to determine how widespread this practice might be. Of course, many crows do remain in the city during the breeding season, and the way such "decisions" are made is little understood. I cannot help projecting, wondering whether any female crows have little corvid nervous breakdowns, stuck for some reason raising their young in Seattle while longing for a more rural nest.

Wherever the chosen nest site turns out to be, the male and the female will both gather materials for the nest and bring them to the site. Both will arrange the sticks into a deep, round, bowl shape, with the large ends on the outside, the narrower ends woven toward the center. Up close, the effect is more intricate, purposeful, and mandala-like than it appears from the street, from which vantage it can look like something of an ill-planned mess. In pairs where I have been able to distinguish male from female, I have noticed that the female manages most of the fine-tuning in the arrangement of nest sticks, and I have further observed that she will accomplish much of this secretly, after the male is satisfied with the placement of his stick and has flown off to gather more. She will watch him leave, then move his most recent addition to suit her more delicate tastes. I do exactly the same thing with Tom when arranging furniture in the living room or art on the wall. He'll think we're finished and then I'll modify. More often, I'll feign contentment in the interest of marital bliss, then institute my refinements after Tom leaves the room. I have watched the same nest-building behavior among Pied-billed Grebes and wondered if it might be somewhat widespread, perhaps with a biological basis. We females normally have to brood the young, after all. It makes sense that we would be fussier about what sticks were poking us where.

After the branchlets for the exterior of the nest are arranged to everyone's satisfaction, the interior is fashioned, and it is another matter altogether. Most people have never seen the inside of a crow's nest, but it is worth making the effort to do so. Once it is clear that the crows are no longer using the nest—anytime after the end of summer would be safe—go ahead and climb up to one.* Remember that although enforcement is lax, it is illegal to disturb any nest (besides those of starlings, pigeons, and House Sparrows) or to take one home. Officially, it is not even legal to possess any part of a bird, including a feather, which means most children are minor felons. In any case, although it is a little trouble, it's usually possible to get a glimpse inside a crow's nest, and wholly worthwhile.

Even though eggs have hatched and young have rested, grown, eaten, and defecated at this site for nearly a month, the inside of the nest will be remarkably clean. Eggshells

---

* A surprising number of intelligent adults carry the unexamined, resoundingly false notion that birds live in nests, which of course they do not. Birds lay eggs in nests, and they tend their young there until they fledge. That's it. (The exception is Big Bird, who does seem to sleep in his nest every night.)

are removed by the adults, and baby birds poop in convenient little fecal sacs that are actually eaten by the parents for the first week or two, then picked up and dropped outside the nest. (Ornithologists do not use the word *baby* for birds—humans have babies, birds have *young*—but I think it is a harmless colloquialism.) As the nestlings get older, they learn to hang their little behinds over the side. The nest is lined first with mud, then with anything the enterprising parents can find that will make it soft—stripped bark, moss, bits of string or yarn, weathered paper, occasionally feathers or fur from road-killed rabbits, cats, dogs, possums, deer, or raccoons. (It has become a sign of eco-commitment to leave one's dryer lint out to be gathered by birds for nest linings. Dryer lint is soft and pleasant, and it is obvious why this might seem like a good idea, but it is not. Residue from detergent and dryer sheets can be irritating and toxic to naked young birds, and dryer lint tends to hold moisture exceedingly well, which can make the nest wet and cold, and actually increase mortality.) The crow's nest is a remarkably intricate piece of work, belying both the rough exterior of the structure and the bulkiness of its creators.

Copulation may take place at any time before, during, or after the nest building. Extensive courtship displays are rare in crows, probably because they mate for life, so attracting a mate is, most years, unnecessary. But pairs do actively work to maintain their bond, and even an inexperienced watcher can get a sense of what's going on between a crow couple. Pairs walk together and sit next to each other in trees, on electrical wires, and at the nest. They engage in allopreening, gently nipping each other at the back of the neck, the base of the bill, and the corners of the eyes. They whisper to each other, especially as dusk settles, in a kind of pillow talk. Many of these intimate behaviors—closeness, allopreening, and special murmurs—will eventually be shared with the young, as in primate families.

Most of us have probably seen a precopulatory display between crows at some point during the spring. Both male and female will crouch, flatten their heads, flutter their wings, and vibrate their tales (sometimes the male will do these things alone and the female will add a begging call—a nasal *waaah* of the sort given by begging young throughout the summer). The female holds flat and still while the male mounts her, jumping on her back and wrapping his tail around to fit his cloacal protuberance—the sex organ specially enlarged for the season—into her cloacal opening. Copulation takes only seconds. During the period of sexual receptivity, the male will guard his mate carefully, as unmated males occasionally swoop in to attempt extra-pair copulations. Such males are attacked by the "rightful" mate, and perhaps other males in the area, and are resisted by the female, sometimes with a great deal of sincerity, sometimes with less. During the "cloacal kiss," the male may flap his wings for balance, and the female sometimes emits an unpleasantly loud, hoarse, croaking sound, audible at a good distance. Most of the time, she is quiet. Crows are not ones to luxuriate in post-cloacal bliss; within seconds the birds resume the activities of the day, picking worms, or gathering materials for the nest.

Before nesting, the female develops a brood patch—she loses a patch of feathers on her belly, and the area becomes highly vascularized for warming the eggs. A bird's brood patch is a wondrous place, hot, moist, and pulsing with the promise of protection and of life. The female is fed by the male at the nest, taking occasional breaks to preen, stretch, or make a quick flight around the neighborhood. The male, through all of this, guards the nest vigilantly. This is the time when I receive phone calls from all manner of friend and acquaintance, asking why they are being dive-bombed by crows. Curiously, most people fail to notice that the behavior is seasonal. They think it is something that crows just *do,* and I have to point out that they were not being dive-bombed a month ago, and in two months or so, they will be safe again.

Crow eggs are a species of blue—anywhere from a pale ice-blue to a darker turquoise-blue. Birds that nest in the shade almost always have blue eggs; the eggs are a quieter presence in the gray light, not brightly obvious as white eggs would be. White eggs are typical of birds that nest in cavities or some other place where their eggs are not easy to spot, and so color is no issue. Crow eggs are smooth, smoother than a chicken's, and variably spotted with dark red-brown pigment, sometimes with just a few spots on one end, sometimes with so many spots and streaks that hardly any blue shows through. Many kinds of birds have spotted eggs; the spots break up the color of the egg for camouflage (again, the eggs of cavity nesters, which are never seen, rarely have spots). Eggs do not grow spotted, but have spots "applied" as they pass through the oviduct, sliding against special pigment-laden pores (which is why the markings so often look streaky).

Crows are as secretive as a big black bird can be as they construct their nests, but because they build in early spring, when the trees are not yet fully leafed-out—usually in March, though sometimes in February (in warmer climes) or as late as April (in colder)—we can usually see where they fly with their sticks and, if we are nonchalant about it, observe the process. If the crows catch on that we are watching, they will become uncomfortable in the extreme. They will look every which way while clutching their stick in their bill, crouch, appear confused about where to go (surely not to the nest!), perhaps drop the stick to "Caw! Caw!" and fly off. They will sometimes even go to a tree some distance from their nest and pretend to build there. But if you act as if you do not see the crows, as if you were passing along in any case and are only pausing to check the time, or rearrange the groceries in your backpack, or just enjoy the sky-blue day, you might be allowed to watch them proceed to their real nest. In the next few weeks, the nest will be finished, the laying of the clutch will begin, the crows will become even more secretive, and the leaves growing on the trees will obscure our view, so this is a good time to watch.

Crows themselves, it seems, learn a great deal from watching other crows. It is a sign of their intelligence and social complexity that crows are among the few nonhuman animal groups to have a "helper" at the nest. Very often, in addition to the two parents, another fully grown crow will be constantly present at the nest, helping to feed the young, watching over them, and sometimes guarding the nest in the parents' absence like a live-in crow nanny. While most songbirds breed in the year after they hatch, crows wait until they are three or four, and the helper is usually one of these pre-nesters, between one and four years old and most likely a relative of one of the parents—a cousin, niece, or young from a previous year. For years it was assumed that nests with helpers in attendance were more successful and fledged more young. But this turns out not to be true; nests with helpers fledge about the same percentage of young as nests without helpers. What recent studies do suggest, though, is that birds that worked as helpers themselves have a higher fledging rate when it comes their turn to nest. By watching and helping, they learn to become more attentive parents.

With this is mind, I turn back to my own disgruntled helper at the nest, who, in spite of her scowl, trots dutifully behind me, handing me clothespins as I hang the load of lightly colored things out to dry in the warm spring air. I can almost smell the smoke as Claire's question stews and brews in her nine-year-old brain. Knowing that she herself is learning by watching the habits that might inform her own future household, and perhaps those of generations to come, I feel the clothespin in my hand grow suddenly hot and ominous. My little crow's seemingly simple question is a good and deep one. Why am I doing this? We talk about voting and other cases where a seemingly small action has wider resonance. We talk about ethics: when we know what we ought to do, what difference does it make what anyone else does? Whence does our action properly spring, from knowledge of a certain outcome, or from doing what we believe is true and good and beautiful? We talk about how satisfying it is to accomplish something using just the sun and no machine at all. We talk about how other people might notice what we are doing and decide to do it themselves. We talk about how pleasant it is to be outside with clean, wet laundry, how good and stiff it feels when we bring it in, and how the wooden clothespins make such a nice "tink" when dropped in the bag. Claire remains skeptical about the global ramifications of our activities but has nevertheless become a clothesline evangelist, touting the ecological and philosophical good of the line and the plight of the salmon to all and sundry, including the woman at Target buying dryer sheets in the middle of a sunny spring day. In the end we leave the question *why?* an open one, as indeed it must remain.

If I could draw a line for her, I would—a line between our lives, our homes, our habits, and wild nature. *Here,* here at this point, our actions spill out into "nature," into the earth. *Here* they remain contained. In a time of ecological crisis, our boundaries would be so much clearer, our responsibilities laid bare. We could keep to our circle and launch spirited crusades to "save" the rest. But our homey thresholds are flimsy and marginal. They represent the point from which we cross into nature and—distressingly, sometimes—the point at which nature crosses back. No matter how mightily we maintain our fortresses, they remain shockingly semipermeable. Our tidy interiors are visited regularly by spiders, bees, carpenter ants, molds, House Sparrow nests in the rafters, and squirrels in the attic. There is rain that comes in, dust, shafts of light, the disembodied wings of dragonflies. Now and then a bird. Less frequently a bat.* My friend Melanie left cat food inside the back door and discovered a raccoon eating it. My sister found a possum in her bathroom. In Africa and India, where the homes are open to allow for a flow of air against impossible heat, they are regularly ransacked by the abundant crows.

We show scarcely any more respect for the boundaries we erected ourselves. We eat food that comes from the soil, the sun, the sky, and we shit back into the sewer. We are incapable of isolation. Every time we sip wine, feed the cat, order pizza, watch *Survivor,* every time we do anything, anything at all, we are brushing, however surreptitiously, however beneath our awareness—however, even, against our

---

* Most people become agitated in the extreme when a flying vertebrate enters the house. It is something to be ready for, as nearly everyone will have some sort of bird in the house at some time in their life. If a bird comes inside, open all the windows and doors; the bird will fly, like a dying thing seeking deliverance, toward the light. If you have a window that doesn't open, pull the curtains over it so the bird won't fly into it and break her neck. If all seems to go awry and the bird ends up falling into a corner huddled and exhausted, then calmly walk over and drop a light cloth over her, gently pick her up, and release her outside. Refrain from indulging in a poetic tossing of the bird into the air, where it might leap into glorious flight. After enduring the stress of captivity, birds need a moment to collect themselves before returning to their freedom. Place the bird in a quiet place, or in the palm of your hand if you like, where you can observe her closely, and feel her heart beat and her gathering strength. You can pretend that she is sitting there because she likes you and knows you are helping her, rather than because she is scared witless and has forgotten, for a moment, what to do, before she suddenly flies.

will—a wilder, natural world. Such awareness is simultaneously daunting and beautiful. It means that everything we do matters, and matters wondrously. More than we thought, more than we can even know. Yes, of course we must do all of the things we now know by rote: we must replace our incandescent lightbulbs with compact fluorescents, and recycle, and compost, and ride our bikes, and buy organic, local, biointensive, fair-trade. All of it. And if we can manage these things with a joyful heart, then all the better. But this is not about checklists, is it? About the reduction of our planetary relationships to a mean tally of resources used, saved, and available? It is about a habit of being, a way of knowing, a way of dwelling. It is about attentive recognition of our constant, inevitable continuity with life on earth, and the gorgeous knowledge this entails. There is a crow's nest in the neighbor's yard, and there are feathers at our feet. We walk around like poems—our lives infused with meaning beyond themselves.

Six

HELPING

An Uncertain Grace

*What is kind and what is wild do not contradict
each other. Kindness is not a characteristic lauded by
modernity. At best it is portrayed as a pastel quality,
something meek and mild: tame. At worst, it is foolish.
A naïve characteristic in this dog-eat-dog world. To me,
it is the opposite. Kindness is both wild and wise.*

— JAY GRIFFITHS

One late spring morning, I was awakened at five a.m.
by a discordant rush of crow calls that could only
be interpreted as meaning two things at once: "displaced
chick!" and "predator!" Though the scolding could have been
directed at a dog, cat, human, or hawk, raccoon was my best
guess for that hour of the day. Given the time of year, I had
been waiting for just such a clatter. I rushed downstairs and
out into the brisk morning, where the story was laid bare.
One adult crow hovered on a wire overhead, scolding to beat
hell. Another adult crow was dive-bombing a raccoon, which
was attempting to make its lumbering getaway. It was one
of our regular neighborhood raccoons—the huge one with
half a tail. Crows always keep a reproachful eye on raccoons,
but the raccoons do not usually inspire quite so much rancor.
It didn't take long to find out the reason for this morning's
enthusiasm. There in the middle of the street sat a fat, quiet,
wide-eyed baby crow.

Aware that any respectable natural historian would

refrain from calling young birds *babies,* I found I could not in this instance help myself. A young bird stands up straight with a tail at least half grown, and flappingly begs without falling over. A young bird flies hither and yon, even if it doesn't do so very well and hasn't perfected its landing. But this bird was a *baby.* About three minutes ago it was probably still a nestling. It had fits of downy gray fluff sticking out from under its disheveled black feathers. Its tail was nothing but a nubbin. It looked as if the world was all too bright and shiny and hurt its eyes. It stood in the middle of the street, gazing slowly to and fro, with no earthly idea that there is such a thing as a crow-squishing car that uses this street as a path. It provoked every maternal instinct in my bones.

I crouched down, crawled right up to the little fluff, and looked him in the eye. Fledgling crows have light blue eyes with dark brown irises, nothing like the dark amber eye of the adult crow. "Out of the road, little one," I whispered. The crow sweetly tipped his head. In just a few more hours this bird will have lived enough to learn a proper wariness in the presence of a large mammal such as myself. His post-nest amazement will be undiminished, but he will have just enough sense to hop briskly away. Now he just naively stared. I shoved him bodily out of the road, pushing his feathered little bottom along until he rested beneath some shady shrubbery.

It's fledging season—the few weeks each summer that find young birds leaping exuberantly from their nests, though they are often quite unable to fly. For days before they actually jump, you can see the small birds readying themselves.

They cling to the edge of the nest with outstretched wings, teetering as they practice flapping. Sometimes the nestlings step cautiously out of the nest, line themselves up along a branch and sidestep back and forth along it for a day or two, gathering courage before taking the big leap. Twice I have seen an adult encourage a ready-but-reluctant chick out of the nest and onto the branch by placing food a foot or so beyond the young bird's reach.

When the young crows finally do jump, they are often not at all ready for flight. They flap wildly as they crash to earth, where they crouch wide-eyed over their fat bellies, dazed and astonished. It is an anxious few days, between fledging and flight, when the young birds are exceedingly vulnerable and tended closely by their parents.

Many people tell me that they have never seen a young crow, which is unlikely to be true. Most of the time the fat little chicks such as the one in our road are well hidden by their parents, and not easy to get a look at unless you have your eye on a nest. But slightly older chicks, ones that really are ready to leave the nest, or have just learned to fly, or are later in their hatch-year, as it's called, are all over the place; we see them throughout the summer and into the fall. The problem is that we equate youngness with small- ness, a mistake when it comes to most birds. Once they have fledged, birds are typically about the same size as an adult, even though they are only a month or two old. The young of many avian species are recognizable by their plum- age. Young robins, for example, have spotted breasts, and starlings are mousy brown all over, not shimmery black like the adults. Crows are a trickier case because they are pretty much all black in all plumages—male, female, young, old. But there are all kinds of ways to tell a young crow from an adult. Hatch-year birds, though blackish overall, have a brown tinge to their feathers, especially noticeable on the back, and their plumage is dull, not shiny and iridescent like an adult crow's. If they are very young, they might still have a touch of downy fluff here and there, most likely right above the eye. They might have a pinkish fleshy patch at the corner of the bill. This is a remnant of the *gape,* or bright mouth lining that glows up at the parents when chicks tilt their heads back and open their mouths wide (called *gaping*), inspiring the adult to drop in a nice worm. Chicks of different species have different-colored gapes. A robin's is red, a wren's orange, and a crow's is pink. At the time a young crow leaves the nest, its tail will be short and stubby, and it'll stay that way for at least a couple of weeks. But the very best way to tell a young bird is by its behavior. Young birds are awkward fliers. For several days or a week, they flap clumsily around in the branches of a tree, and if they fall to the ground, they might not be able to get back up. Soon they will learn to fly a little better, following their parents around and incessantly begging for food, but their landings are likely to be terrible for a couple of months.

Beyond flight, there are several behaviors that are dead giveaways for crows that are between a few weeks and a few months old. Freshly fledged crows are not stupid—they possess all the native intelligence of their species—but they *are* naive. They stand around looking at things. They hear a

cat with a bell on its collar and wonder what that nice tinkling sound might be. They stand in traffic. They look at
you sweetly, and blink. Like other intelligent young animals,
they like to play. Adult crows play too, but not for as long or
as creatively as the young.

A few years ago, when we lived in a cottage not far from
our new house, a nestful of crows leapt from their birthplace
in our ancient apple tree onto the ground beneath it. There
were four fledglings, which is a very successful nest, two
adults, and one other adult, presumably a helper. None of
the young could fly, and as our yard was surrounded by a
high fence, the young crows were pretty much stuck on the
ground. As they grew stronger and more comfortable over
the next few days, they began to entertain themselves by dis-
mantling my garden. A litter of Labrador puppies couldn't
have been more destructive. The fledglings pulled up the
low bent-willow fence I had painstakingly made to outline
the beds; the twigs were tied together at the bottom with
twine, and they just grabbed on to the loose string ends and
pulled them out. They uprooted all my seedling carrots, not
wildly, but slowly, neatly, and with concentration, as if working on their knitting. They laid the seedlings in rows. Finishing one crop, they'd move on to another. When they got
to my beautiful Kentucky Blue pole beans, I decided it was
time to defend the harvest. I turned on the hose, and ever
so gently (they were only babies, after all) sprayed it at the
chicks, hoping to establish some kind of aversion to the garden area. Instead, all four of them gathered under the spray,
flapped their wings, and opened their bills, in what appeared

to be absolute joy. I laughed, but in that slightly imbalanced way that could turn into crying if someone looked at me the wrong way. And then I gave up. We would shop at the farmer's market this year, and enjoy our terrible young guests while we could. Meanwhile, I brought the hose out for them several more times in the next few days.

The escape reaction is established in young crows at about twenty-five days after hatching, a week or so before they leave the nest. This means that a chick in a nest will not normally be frightened of a human. If you make scratching sounds, or give their bill a little rub, a baby crow (and most other baby birds) will gape at you, begging food. But after about three weeks, they will normally cower and try to get away. I can only guess that these crows didn't run from me because I had been observing them so closely since their hatching. Both they and their parents must have become so accustomed to my near-constant presence that they didn't respond with alarm when I approached them, not even when I had a hose.

As long as they are out of harm's way, it is best to pay no attention at all to nestlings of most avian species. The presence of solicitous humans will keep the parent birds from tending their young, and will also invite the attention of predators, such as cats. I relax this rule the tiniest bit in the case of crows. Crows become peevish in the extreme if their young are put under observation, but overall, urban crows have adjusted well to a certain level of human disturbance and compensate by making themselves loud, large, and conspicuous, as well as by feigning fearlessness. It is unlikely that a bit of cautious crow chick–watching will do much harm.

About an hour after the excitement with the crows and the raccoon and the chick in the road, I took a little meander up the sidewalk to see where the crow family was hanging out. Wanting to maintain good crow relations and to refrain from upsetting the adults unnecessarily, I affected nonchalance, as if I were just out for a stroll, like Winnie the Pooh and the bees. Right when I spotted the fledgling up the street, another bird just his size jumped out from beneath a neighbor's vine maple. Clearly I'd startled her, and she was trying to flop away from me. Her left leg was dangling to the side, bent. Without thinking much about it, I scooped up the injured baby bird and toted her home, ignoring the adult crow's fervent scolding and dive-bombing. Having worked as a wildlife rehabilitator, I've raised perhaps a hundred fledgling birds, including several injured young crows. My response was almost involuntary, and not at all well-thought-out. Certainly I had no idea that this bird, the not-yet-named Charlotte, would become such a fixture in my yard and my life.

The bird's left tarsometatarsus—the bone between the backward-bending leg joint that birds have and the "foot"—was broken, or at least horribly bent. Baby bird bones are highly cartilaginous, more bendable than an adult bird's and less brittle. They tend not to break cleanly, but they do mangle. I covered the chick's eyes to calm her as I carried her inside, placed her quietly in a newspaper-lined box in the bathtub, and closed the door. I could feel her keel, the breastbone that sticks out on birds to accommodate the large pectoral muscles required for flight, sticking sharply through the skin. She wasn't as fat as a fresh fledgling should be. I broke off the end of a popsicle stick (from an actual popsicle) for a splint, and sanded down the edge. I picked up the bird, looked her over for other injuries, and found small open cuts on the bottom of her right foot. I wrapped her in a dish towel to discourage fidgeting, and kept her eyes covered with the towel's corner to keep her from being afraid. I didn't see any signs of cat bites or scratches on her body and assumed she had just had a bad landing when she jumped from the nest. She sat quietly while I cleaned the cuts and rubbed them with antibiotic. The break was in an easily splintable place. I positioned the leg against the popsicle stick, wrapped it in tidy layers of gauze, and covered it all with that stretchy first-aid tape that clings to itself rather than to skin (or leg scales or feathers). I was careful that no gauze stuck out for the crow to pick at. I admired my work. It was a good splint, and the bird could rest neatly on her haunches without the broken leg splaying. I put water on the stove to hard-boil an egg (for the crow), and wondered what to do.

It is generally believed that the most ecologically advanced position is to let nature take its course. But I am not convinced that this is, in fact, always the highest course of action, or that it is ever entirely clear exactly what nature's course might be. What happens when an injured bird crosses the path of a human? Typically, humans encounter injured birds in places where humans walk. Yards, garden paths, parks, sidewalks, roads, woodland trails—places exhibiting some degree of human interference that remove them from the mythological place where we imagine Pure Nature to reside. But let's say the bird was found in a place that satisfies even the most romantic vision of Nature. Does the arrival of a human change a situation, as if by magic, into non-nature? And if we allow that our presence might be deemed "natural," does this concession last only as long as we keep our hands tied behind our backs? Or are we allowed the spectrum of activity typical of the human animal? What is nature's course?

For better or for worse, the animal with whom the injured bird now shares company is a complex one—one capable of scientific analysis, one that might be prone to ecological understanding, but one whose most remarkable capacities, whose saving grace, is of a higher order. This is a human animal, who can not only think well but also feel, quite deeply, compassion for other beings, including nonhumans, particularly if they are hurt. To think that it somehow shows greater intellectual discernment to stuff compassion away for the sake of scientific distance is an error, one that does not sufficiently allow the range of the human animal's complexity. We can think and feel compassion at the same time. We can act on this compassion without forsaking our intelligence. To believe otherwise is a myth of pure humanistic materialism.

It is good to be moved to help, just as it is difficult to know what "help" might be. Most people cannot even tell an injured bird from a noninjured bird, and it is at this basic point that the best of intentions begin to go awry. Crows often go into a kind of torpor and lie on the ground with their bills half-open when sunning themselves, looking to all the world as if they are about to succumb to some terrible malady. Robins become drunk when they eat fermented mountain ash berries, and in this state can be gathered up into our hands. Fledglings of all species often jump from the nest before they can fly; on the ground they are floppy, uncoordinated, dazed, and unwary. People commonly believe them to be "sick." Such birds are looked after by their parents as they flop helplessly about for a day or three, but even a bird as bold as a crow will not tend its fledgling with a human (no matter how well-meaning, or how well the human believes itself to be hidden) lurking in the vicinity. Such misunderstanding leads all too many birds to be proclaimed orphans and made into some well-intended but horrific bird-raising project for human children—a "learning activity" that inevitably ends in disaster, both ornithological and emotional.

Global avian populations are perilously declining because of human-wrought habitat degradation, and many individual avian injuries are at root human-caused. So if we can assist a wild bird wisely by, say, putting a fledgling out of harm's way (just pick it up and put it in a tree—birds cannot "smell human" on their chicks, and even if they could, they would not abandon their young) or by delivering an injured bird to a wildlife clinic, then we ought to do so. But what about crows?

Most crow populations are increasing. There is no ecological balance to set right here, as in the case of many other avian species. Indeed, if anything, letting the crow die would probably be the most ecologically enlightened move. Crows living in the urban landscape reap the benefits of easy food and shelter, and their populations are barely checked by cars, cats, and other urban and suburban hazards. Urban crow life is dangerous and scrappy, but it all works out, and the crows, as a group, seem to come out on top.

Still, once an injured crow has entered one's sphere, particularly if one knows just what to do to help it, the decision becomes more complicated. And now I had a crow in a box in my bathtub. My decision to rush out and grab the crow had been almost instinctual. I have raised several young crows. Some of them were siblings, and so they had a kind of community—upon release they could be crows together, and they seemed to do fine. Another of "my" crows was killed and eaten by a cat or some other predator within two days of release. I found its banded leg just yards from where I let it go and promptly threw up. One of them was killed by a neighbor: lacking appropriate wariness around humans, it landed on her deck railing, dangerously close to her toddler, as she perceived it, and she beat it to death with a broom. I have since learned that such a death for human-raised crows is not at all uncommon. And the last of my crows ended up who-knows-how. I raised these crows not by personal choice, exactly, but because people knowing my background had brought them to me over the years and there seemed no good way to put them back.

I peek in on the bathtub crow. If I put her back outside, she's basically toast. This is a neighborhood full of cats and raccoons, cars, and marauding small children. I saw a Cooper's Hawk overhead yesterday. The chick is already thin, and even for a robust, two-legged fledgling, survival is a wary, uncertain prospect. But if I keep the crow in the box, feed her, heal her foot, and successfully release her, she's still, in all likelihood, toast. If it were nearly any other sort of bird, this is the course I would probably take, but there is another element of crow life that makes their rehabilitation far more complex than that of most avian species. That is the crow social life.

Birds raised by humans tend to be shunned by crow society—the essential crow life-support system that allows birds to find and share food, roosts, mates, protection from predators, and general crow good times. Without it, and coupled with a lack of proper wariness of humankind, these crows don't last long. At least outside, the injured crow will be tended by her parents, helped as a young crow is meant to be helped. They will watch her, scold anything that comes near her, and attack anything that comes *very* near. They will bring her grasshoppers, spiders, fruits and vegetables, perhaps a frog, a mouse, a bit of roadkill. They will soak her food in water before feeding it to her, keeping her hydrated whether or not she herself remembers to drink. In a few weeks, though she will still hunch and flutter and beg, they will gradually begin to ignore her, and she will learn to find food for herself. Perhaps the adults will be aware of her injury and will be less hurried about moving her into independence, guarding, preening, feeding her more indulgently than they do the healthy chick. With the bent leg, she has a slim possibility of survival (a broken wing would be another story). Her good right leg could grow strong enough to support her, and she might learn to fly. But it's a long shot and a difficult choice.

While the egg was boiling I listened to NPR. Our government had been proclaiming "progress" in war-torn Iraq, but by the time I had decided what to do with the crow, I learned that a fresh round of suicide bombings had killed dozens of civilians. In his journal, Thomas Merton wrote, "Someone will say: you worry about birds. Why not worry about people?" He answered unapologetically, "I worry about *both* birds and people. We are in the world and part of it, and we are destroying everything because we are destroying ourselves spiritually, morally, and in every way. It is all part of the same sickness, it all hangs together." The broken thing on our doorstep? We pick it up and bind its leg. Our gesture resonates against an unnatural sense of isolation. But even our acts of compassion ought to be appropriate, if we can manage that. We work to make them *right*.

I make the crow a meal of high-protein cat food (dog food is better, but I only have a cat) mixed with blackberries and half of a crushed multivitamin. In another bowl, I mash the yolk of the egg with a little of the white. The bird is too freaked out to eat, so I wrap her in the towel again and shove this delicious, nutritious meal down her throat, allowing her time to swallow after each bite. "Here you go, Charlotte," I hear myself say, though I didn't consciously intend to name her. I regretfully unwrap the splint and apply a little more antibiotic. I take the crow outside, making sure that her parents see me. I place her under a protected shrub, and cover her eyes gently with my hand until she is calm. I say a little prayer for the highest good, whatever it is, and leave her there.

Seven

SEEING

The Monk, the Professor, and the Sense of Wonder

Go to nature; take the facts into your own hands; look,
and see for yourself.

— Louis Agassiz, as recalled by William James

I have been studying the same dead crow at my desk for three hours. I will take a lunch break, then continue to work for four more hours. I studied this bird for seven hours yesterday and will strive for seven more tomorrow. I am beginning to think this is too strenuous a project for someone who was so recently walking around in pajamas all day and worry that I might begin losing my mind, one dulled black feather at a time. I try to remember: *Why am I doing this?*

In 1859, the hopeful young naturalist Samuel Scudder entered the laboratory of renowned zoologist Louis Agassiz in Harvard's new Museum of Comparative Zoology. What followed is one of the best stories in all of natural history. Agassiz, broadly built, slightly unkempt in spite of his frock coat, and uncontainably jovial, sat Scudder kindly in a chair and asked him a few questions about his object, his background, and how he proposed to put the knowledge he might acquire to use, should he be accepted as a student. When asked if there was any particular branch of zoology to which he hoped to devote himself, Scudder replied with enthusiasm. He wished very specially to be an entomologist, to study insects. And when did he wish to begin? "Now," was Scudder's unhesitating reply. He describes the scene that followed:

> [My answer] seemed to please him, and with an energetic "Very well!" he reached from a shelf a huge jar of specimens in yellow alcohol. "Take this fish," he said, "and look at it; we call it a *haemulon;* by and by I will ask what you have seen." With that he left me, but in a moment returned with explicit instructions as to the care of the object entrusted to me.

Agassiz would be remembered by many for his absolute insistence on respect for specimens of any kind—animal, botanical, geological. "No man is fit to be a naturalist," he told Scudder, "who does not know how to take care of specimens." Scudder was to keep the fish in a metal tray and occasionally moisten its surface with spirits from the jar, always carefully replacing the cork stopper.

Scudder could not help but be somewhat disappointed, for "gazing at a fish did not commend itself to an ardent entomologist." In ten minutes, Scudder had "seen all of the fish," and started out in search of the professor, who had, much to his dismay, left the museum. So he went back to his little room and lingered over the odd and sundry specimens stored on the dusty shelves. Eventually, he turned in horror back to his own *haemulon,* which was now entirely dry! He "dashed the fluid over the fish as if to resuscitate the beast from a fainting fit, and looked with anxiety for a return of the normal sloppy appearance." With this "little excitement" over, there was nothing to be done but return to his mute companion. A half hour passed, then an hour: "The fish began to look loathsome. I turned it over and around; looked it in the face—ghastly; from behind, beneath, above, sideways, at a three-quarters' view—just as ghastly. I was in despair."

At last a "happy thought" dawned. He could *draw the fish*. Armed with a pencil, Scudder immediately began to "discover new features in the creature," just as Professor Agassiz returned. "That is right," the naturalist spoke encouragingly, "a pencil is one of the best of eyes. I am glad to notice, too, that you keep your specimen wet, and your bottle corked." After the encouraging words regarding pencils and wetness, Professor Agassiz added, "Well, what is it like?" Scudder recalled what happened next:

> He listened attentively to my brief rehearsal of the structure of parts whose names were still unknown to me: the fringed gill-arches and movable *operculum;* the pores of the head, fleshy lips and lidless eyes; the lateral line, the spinous fins and forked tail; the compressed and arched body. When I finished, he waited as if expecting more, and then, with an air of disappointment, "You have not looked carefully, why," he continued more earnestly, "you haven't even seen one of the most conspicuous features of the animal, which is as plainly before your eyes as the fish itself; Look again, look again!" and he left me to my misery.

Naturally Scudder was mortified. "Still more of that wretched fish!" But he returned to the task with renewed purpose and discovered several previously unseen features of the fish, and then several more. He came to realize that the professor's criticism had indeed been just. The next hours passed more quickly, and before leaving for the night, the professor poked his nose in and inquired, "Do you see it yet?" "No," Scudder answered, "I am certain I do not, but I see how little I saw before." "That is next best," said the famed teacher earnestly, "but I won't hear you now; put away your fish and go home; perhaps you will be ready with a better answer in the morning. I will examine you before you look at the fish."

Well, this was disconcerting. Now Scudder had to think about that fish all night long, without being able to check his poor memory against the thing itself. Professor Agassiz put him at ease the next morning with the warmth of his greeting. He seemed honestly anxious that his pupil see in the fish what he himself could see. "Do you perhaps mean," Scudder offered tentatively, "that the fish has symmetrical sides with paired organs?" "Of course! Of course!" cried Agassiz with heartfelt pleasure. He proceeded to discourse "most happily and enthusiastically" on the significance of such a structure, and when he slowed, Scudder asked aloud what he should do next. "Oh!" came the unhesitating answer, "look at your fish!"

There are countless tales of students subjected to Agassiz's Zen-master teaching techniques, locked in rooms with nothing but a turtle carapace or lobster shell or oyster specimen, and not allowed out until they could give an account of the natural truths the object possessed. Those who discovered the secrets were initiated into further naturalist's training, and those who didn't were "blotted from the book of honor and of life." Testimonials from the unblotted tell of how dear these hard-wrought lessons became, extending to all of their future studies and informing their chosen field. Agassiz's students learned the value of comparing specimens, which was then the foundation of a naturalist's work; they learned to depend on the rounded fullness of organisms, rather than learning from a book; they learned that "facts are stupid," as Agassiz liked to repeat, "until brought into connection with some general law"; and they learned how to form proper questions, ones that might use concrete observation to reveal overarching tendencies and truths. As a young man, William James traveled extensively with Agassiz in Brazil, studying tropical ecology. "I remember that I often put questions to him about the facts of our new tropical habitat, but I doubt if he ever answered one of these questions of mine outright. He always said: 'There, you see you have a definite problem. Go and Look, and find the answer for yourself.'"*

---

* As delightful as such stories are, and as brilliant a naturalist as Agassiz appears to have been, his scientific legacy will always be blemished. By the time of his death in 1873, Louis Agassiz had reshaped scientific education, spoken out as a proponent of women's equality and education, and become Harvard's most celebrated and best-loved professor, and was America's foremost naturalist. But Agassiz was, like many scientists and politicians of his time, undeniably racist. His 1851 *Essay on*

Lacking Agassiz himself, but wanting to benefit as best I could from his methods, I placed a prepared (that is, stuffed) study skin of an adult male crow on my desk. My intention was to observe the specimen for three days—a total of twenty-one hours. That might be paltry by Agassizian standards, but it seemed like a reasonably stringent goal for me and my still-delicate, recently toppled brain.

First, I closed the curtains. The crow wire is outside my window, and crows do not take well to seeing the dead bodies of their colleagues. Their reaction is not predictable, but it often takes one of two tacks. Seeing a dead crow, other crows will avoid for a good long while the place where the corpse appeared—ranging from hours to weeks and sometimes even years. Alternatively, they will converge in a great group of boisterous madness, flocking in numbers, landing on the wires and branches, shrieking and scolding, then suddenly and utterly disappearing, leaving an eerie, overfull silence. In this scenario, again they will often vacate a place for days, weeks, months, or years. Sometimes, if the

---

Classification defined earthly climate zones by which he believed all animals, plants, and human races could be classified. Slaveholders repeated his beliefs in support of their own. Though he became a vocal abolitionist, Agassiz never abandoned his belief that humans were defined by race, and that blacks were inferior. In addition, Agassiz, twenty-five years after publication of the *Origin of Species,* and in spite of the evolutionary ramifications of much of his own biological work, took his general opposition to Darwinian natural selection to his grave. Of Darwin's work he spoke with unaccountable indifference: "The world has arisen in some way or other. How it originated is the great question, and Darwin's theory, like all other attempts to explain the origin of life, is thus far merely conjectural."

crows know what happened to the dead crow—exactly how it became a corpse—they will not worry so much. If they saw it get hit by a car, for example, they might be more wary of cars for a while, but they will not avoid the site.

At other times, they will become very upset over the cause of death. An acquaintance of mine told me that in order to "discourage" the abundant crows in their yard, her son killed one of them with his gun and hung the dead bird from their basketball hoop (I didn't think to ask what kind of gun a teenage boy was toting around a Seattle backyard, though now I wonder). Twenty crows, she says, swirled in, cawing angrily for more than an hour before disappearing. The tactic ended up working: the crows permanently abandoned the yard. (And her conclusion? That *crows* are evil.) In any case, I did not want to be associated with dead crows in the eyes of the birds I study.

I could almost hear Agassiz speaking to me from behind his Victorian curls, his lace cuffs stinking of preserving spirits. "Look at the crow." After just ten minutes, I felt exactly like Professor Scudder and started peeking around the room for something else to think about. Surely I knew that crow from tip to tail. I remembered Scudder's missteps, and imagined very well Professor Agassiz's disappointment, but instead of redoubling my efforts, I assured myself that a *haemulon* must be a far more complex being, at least topographically, than a crow, making Scudder's task simpler than the one I set myself. It was fine for him to look for hours and hours—certainly he had more to see. Here was just a heap of black feathers. I thought I might check my e-mail but instead remembered the pencil exhortation and went back to the crow for an hour, pencil in hand; I ended up sketching quite happily. Soon enough it was five p.m., time for a glass of chardonnay, and (unless something went terribly amiss between now and then) no dead birds until tomorrow.

It might seem an odd, unlikely thing to do, but it is worth keeping an open mind about observing the dead animals that cross our paths, replicating the specimen study that was once so common among nineteenth-century naturalists. Bringing dead birds home is not exactly legal, but I have found that the refrigerator police are not terribly active, and if a pretty bird hits your window, or appears in your parking strip, or is proffered by a neighbor who is privy to your macabre tendencies, then there is really no good reason not to pop it in a Ziploc next to the lemonade concentrate and the Häagen-Dazs for future study. In our freezer, there is a Red Crossbill, a Dunlin, a tiny Rufous Hummingbird, and, sadly, a beautiful adult Cooper's Hawk. (Until recently there was also a Wilson's Warbler, but Claire came to me one day with her friend Laurel and asked, "Mommy, we want to have a funeral for a bird—do you have a dead one?" I was delighted to be able to comply, and the funeral was all that child bird funerals can be, involving a handkerchief-lined box, prayers, hymns, and a grave decorated with tiny stones and flowers.) The birds all lie there stiffly in their Baggies, alongside the one or two crow bodies that come and go (I will replace a ratty one with a nice one, if such comes along). If you have no bird at all, then be on the lookout for something else. Wasps and yellow jackets often die nicely intact, as do beetles, butterflies, and moths. Insects will do as well as anything for this experiment. If you must, you may always resort to a leaf. Truly, any of us can join Scudder as a student of radical vision.*

Finding myself at another psychological impasse with Louis (as the dead crow has come to be known in our household), and seeking further insight, I turn to the medieval monk Saint Benedict, who was conversant with both the vagaries of the human attention span and with crows. Benedict was born in Nursia, north of Rome, sometime about 480 CE. He is best known for writing a monastic rule that still guides the community life of modern monasteries as well as inspiring both the practical and spiritual lives of many laypeople. Even some Buddhist communities rely on the Rule of Saint Benedict, as it is called, though Benedict himself referred to it as his "little rule for beginners"—and it is little, but also chock-full of guidance on how to live simply and well. Not in a cave, as Benedict spent his early hermetic years, but as

---

* I would be remiss if I didn't revise my exhortation to study dead bird specimens in light of the current West Nile virus situation. As I write, two dead crows in my county have tested positive for the virus, and birds, particularly corvids, in other areas of the country are more dramatically affected. Mosquitoes are the vector for West Nile, and it is very difficult for the virus to be transmitted directly from a bird (whether it is dead or alive) to a person. Even so, local health departments now recommend that we do not handle dead birds unless necessary, and if we must, to exercise caution and wear gloves.

nearly all of us live: with others. With meals to cook, with work to do, and with people other than ourselves to look after. With forks that need putting away, linens that need folding, clothes that need replacing, crows on the wire, and guests who drop in. Benedict's writing inspires a commitment to humility, simplicity, and hospitality that is radically countercultural. But Benedict might not have lived to pen his famous Rule had his life not been saved by a crow.

As Benedict's popularity increased, spiritual seekers and would-be monastics came from far and wide to enjoy the presence of the famous monk. A local priest named Florentius, inflamed by jealousy, sent the saint a beautiful loaf of fresh-baked poisoned bread. In Saint Gregory's slender biography of Benedict, a crow is now introduced into the narrative. It "used to come from the forest nearby at the hour when Benedict ate, and it would take some bread from his hand." This means that the monk regularly interacted with a particular crow often enough, gently enough, and over a long enough period of time that he and the crow recognized each other, approached each other closely, and shared a sense of the daily round (including lunch). Unnerved by the poison she perceived in the bread, Benedict's crow presciently plucked the loaf up into her bill, and flew off to dispose of it in the woods before returning, three hours later, for her usual ration from Benedict's hand.

Whenever I study Benedict's Rule, I think of it in this light: as a view of life composed by someone who was not only a monk who thought about how to live well in the earthen community, but was also a companion to crows. It seems that he loved crows, even though they are not quiet or some bright color of yellow or the least bit rare, and even though they don't sing. It means that the most common thing was not beneath his notice.

Saint Benedict writes often of his commitment to the solitary practice of *lectio divina,* and of its necessity in the formation of monks. Literally, *lectio divina* means "reading from God," though it is usually translated as "contemplative" or "spiritual" reading. Terrence Kardong, who interprets the saint's writings almost word-by-word in his exhaustive study *Benedict's Rule,* suggests that the term is not readily translatable and prefers not to render it in English but to leave intact the lilting Latin *lectio divina,* and the practice it speaks to.

Benedict would have his monks choose a particular book—typically a book of Scripture, though the strongly countercultural writings of the desert fathers or mothers, who bore a vital influence upon Benedict, might also do. The student was to read not for comprehension only but also to gain a sense of the inner, secret meaning of the text as it applied to his own life, and to deepen his union with the divine. Never one to sanction the willy-nilly, Benedict insisted that although the monk might take a reasonable length of time to choose the next book he would take up for *lectio* practice, once it was chosen, the monk must commit and read the entire book from start to finish. Slowly. And alone. The book becomes the monastic version of Scudder's *haemulon.*

From the Benedictine sisters at the priory near my home, I have learned the phrase "living *lectio,*" the practice of bringing this kind of attention into other spheres of daily life. I am wary of taking Benedict's *lectio* too far out of context, but I am struck by how apt the language of *lectio* can be for framing good nature study. Particularly if we refuse to be flitty in observation, if we take one question and work on it well over time, this kind of contemplative flow settles upon our watching. I doubt that Benedict would disapprove, and I cannot help but wonder whether his own elucidation of *lectio* practice was in part inspired by his time alone, in nature, without books of any kind, perhaps in the presence of his corvid companions.

Searchingly, I bring all of this to my dead crow. Regarding Agassiz's stringent guidelines, I admit to cheating dreadfully. For one thing, I referred to two specimens rather than one: a stuffed adult male, and a frozen hatch-year bird of indeterminate sex (the sex of the male is known only because his genitals were removed when he was "prepared"). I am sure Agassiz would have allowed me only one bird at a time. I also made ample use of my 10x hand lens, which I know Agassiz discouraged. I tried for one day not using it, and it just seemed silly; there were so many things I wanted to see bigger. And I am not sure whether this is cheating or not, but I am almost certain that Scudder, and other Agassiz students, did not listen to loud music while working, as I often did (Bach and Eddie Vedder). Nor did they sip Tulsi chai tea with plenty of milk and sugar.

In spite of these failures of mind and spirit, I am ready to proclaim my little study a success, though the reasons for this declaration are hardly palpable. Certainly I could make a list of my simple observations. I could note that the black, glossy feathers on the crown and back are outlined with iridescent violet, giving them a scaled appearance, and that these feathers contrast with the feathers on the nape, which are a uniformly flat black. I could write about the fact that the bottom half of the breast feathers, the part that doesn't show, is light gray rather than black (it takes some biological effort to produce dark pigmentation, and if it is not needed because the feathers are not visible, then natural selection does away with it). We see this gray layer when crows stand in the wind and their breast feathers are ruffled. I could talk about how soft crow feathers are. Though the flight apparatus of the wing and tail is rather stiff, the feathers along a crow's mantle, head, and breast are as soft as rabbit fur, and those around the vent (where the poop comes out) are particularly fluffy and remarkably clean. I could mention the bristly but still-soft modified feathers that cover the nostrils and beard the chin, the relative lengths and sharpness of the various toes, how stretched crow skin looks just like a plucked chicken's. I could mention that, like Scudder's *haemulon,* and like my own body, the crow is arranged with rough, beautiful symmetry about a central axis. But I cannot adequately explain why, after just these few hours of corvid *lectio,* I can never look offhandedly at a living crow again. I cannot fully describe how stepping back into normal life, I feel dizzy, trippy, and overcome by the constant, unseen intricacy of living things. But I know there is a name for this.

It is difficult to say *sense of wonder* in this millennial moment, when sleek, cynical, pop-nihilistic writing seems to be a sign of intellectual rigor and rightness. Wonder, as a quality of intellect, has fallen from favor. Too often the word *wonder* is preceded by one of two rather dopey descriptors. We have *childlike* wonder, or we have *wide-eyed* wonder, as if wonder entails a suspension of our intellect. As if, to wonder properly, we have to stand with our mouths agape, waiting for the flies to come in and the drool to ooze out. Grown-up wonder can be just as worthy of the title as that exhibited by a three-year-old. Wonder feeds our best intelligence and is perhaps its source.

In 1956, Rachel Carson wrote an article for the *Woman's Home Companion* titled "Help Your Child to Wonder." In it she both inspired an appreciation for wonder as the primary basis for understanding the natural world properly, and expressed the essentiality of protecting and cultivating this quality as children grow into adulthood:

> If I had influence with the good fairy who is supposed to preside over the christening of all children, I should ask that her gift to each child in the world be a sense of wonder so indestructible that it would last throughout life, as an unfailing antidote against the boredom and disenchantments of later years, the sterile preoccupation with things that are artificial, the alienation from the sources of our strength.

On the lookout for wonder in modern students of natural history, I was struck by a line in Robert Michael Pyle's recent *Sky Time,* where he spoke of the "certainty of wonder in all places." Though this is a lovely sentiment, perhaps it is not quite right. Surely there is the certainty of the *wondrous* in all places. But *wonder* is a response, an attitude of mind and heart, a graced completion of a circle between observer and observed. Wonder is not a given; it is contingent on the habit of being that allows it to arise in the face of the wondrous. This habit is not an accessory for the naturalist, but an essential. When I spoke with Thomas Eisner, the renowned Cornell biologist (also one of the earth's finest naturalists and dearest humans) about his course The Naturalist's Way, I asked him why he had decided to grade the class Pass/Fail. If part of his goal was to bring natural history back into academic favor, then shouldn't the students receive traditional grades? Dr. Eisner, who has had more papers grace the cover of the rigorously academic journal *Science* than any other scientist dead or living, responded simply, "How do you grade wonder?"

We practice wonder by resisting the temptation to hurry past things worth seeing, but it can take work to transcend our preconceived standards for what that worth might be. In the disturbed urban landscape, this is particularly challenging. Unless we happen into a zoo, or unless something goes badly awry, we are not normally going to be seeing bears, cougars, or even deer. Without the hope of a megafaunal sighting to keep us on our toes, our watching must delve one layer, or several, deeper. This is one of the blessings of the urban nature project: without the overtly magnificent to stop us in our tracks, we must seek out the more subversively magnificent. Our sense of what constitutes *wildness* is expanded, and our sense of wonder along with it.

I am glad to leave Louis behind, stretch my legs, and cast my eyes upon the living. Within a couple of blocks, my path crosses a group of crows, foraging on a grassy parking strip. One finds an earthworm, or so I think at first, but I am surprised to see it brace its feet against the earth and extract a fat gray larva. What else lies beneath? The crows, continuing to search for food, turn their heads from side to side, seeing what I cannot. After days with Louis and his cotton-stuffed orbs, these birds' eyes look particularly limpid and intricate.

Vision is the dominant avian sense. The olfactory sense in most birds is not well developed—they smell about as well as a human does. But their large eyes take up so much space in their skulls and fit so tightly that they cannot rotate the oculus as we can, which means they must move their whole heads instead. As predator-scavengers, crows have eyes set toward the front of their heads. A raptor's eyes, requiring full binocular vision for effective hunting, are set even closer together. Many smaller passerines, who must worry about being prey themselves, have eyes placed farther to the sides for better peripheral vision and the tracking of predators that might be sneaking up from behind. When the robin on the lawn cocks her head, she is not listening for worms as she seems to be doing, and as the myth goes. She is turning her head because she has to in order to see the grass.

Birds have sharper vision than any other vertebrates and see, on average, two to three times better than humans. In diurnal birds, the retinas are dense with cones—the same color receptors present in the human retina, though in far fewer numbers—and enhanced by a little-understood physiological system involving pigmented oil droplets, which appear to both sharpen color reception and reduce glare. The backs of avian eyes are flatter than mammals', and the cones are more evenly distributed about the retina, giving birds a broader in-focus field of view. Most birds can also see into the ultraviolet or near-ultraviolet range, making the world, for a bird, a vivid, glowing place. Curiously, corvids seem to be the one passerine group that sees only the violet-spectrum rather than the ultraviolet. Even so, the violet-blue reflectance of their plumage looks far more vibrant to them than it does to us.

For a bird that relies so heavily upon vision, an eye injury can make daily life distressing. I have been observing the patch of shoreline at Alki Beach where the crows meet the Brant, small, beautiful geese with dark-brown-and-cream-colored feathers, dependent on the eelgrass community. Typically, the crows take the area from the waterline upward for their foraging, and the Brant take the waterline outward, though occasionally a Brant will venture out of the lapping wavelets and walk the water's edge. The crows may glance at the goose, assess its distance, and take a step or two back. Most crows ignore the geese. But there is one crow who will not abide the Brant. If a Brant in his radius steps out of the water, he will stretch out his wings and rush at the goose, shrieking at it. Wisely, the Brant always hops back into the water, so I have never been able to find out what the crow would do next if it didn't, though I'm curious. I have watched carefully to determine that it is, in fact, always the same crow that chases the Brant. Turning the scope on him, I discovered that the nictitating membrane (the translucent filmlike covering that birds have to protect their eyes in flight or underwater) of his right eye is always half-closed. He may have some irritation or injury in that eye that affects his vision, so I'm guessing that because he can't see them coming, he is startled when the geese turn up "suddenly" on that side, and this inspires his overblown reaction. It must be frightening to be a half-blind crow.

The crows here on the sidewalk bear little resemblance to the still, understuffed specimen on my desk. But my observation exercise, I know, was anything but futile. These crows are doing nothing extraordinary, but I see them as I never have before. Never so solid, bright, alive. My feet never so secure as on this mossy grass. I recall Thomas Eisner's suggestion: if you want your daughter to remain interested in nature, get her a stereomicroscope. I was amused at this revelation of our biases: where I recommend ever-ready binoculars, Dr. Eisner wants a microscope installed on every kitchen table. But surely we are after the same thing — not just to intensify our everyday way of seeing but to make it normal, habitual, to do so.

Agassiz's exhortation to "look" is really just a preamble. What we are truly called to do with all of this looking is to *see*—to understand, perceive, and register significance and meaning. And why do this? Why work to see? Surely the more we humans comprehend of the earthly life around us, the better chance we have for living intelligently in its midst. But to my mind, one of Benedict's most salient points with respect to *lectio* has to do with its objective—or perhaps its lack of one. Benedict uses the Latin word *vacare*, "to be free for," to refer to the sort of time a monk devotes to *lectio*. It is not work, not "just another labor," but an essential life practice. It matters immensely but does not lead to any practical end. *Lectio* has *meaning*, rather than *purpose*, in any typical material sense. Like bird-watching, it does not drive the economy. We approach it, in Benedict's language, "gladly."

Eight

COEXISTING

FINDING OUR PLACE IN THE ZOÖPOLIS

Yes, creation is moving toward us; life is moving toward
us all the time. We back away, but it keeps pushing
toward us. From radiant space, from luminous darkness,
it is approaching us.

— JOAN HALIFAX

M y parents recently took Claire and me on a walk
to Woodard Bay Conservation Area, a forested trail
leading to a Puget Sound harbor outside Olympia. There
at the beach I found a series of interpretive signs telling a
story called *Crow Sets the Table*, loosely attributed to "northwest native people." In it, the new human creatures who had
come to live at the harbor were starving, and they asked the
wild animals, with whom they were conversant if not actually friendly, for help. Everyone made excuses: Eagle was too
busy minding the pesky jays, Salmon didn't care for anyone
without fins, and Bear was getting sleepy as the cold weather
came on. Only Crow offered. "I will help these people," he
said. Crow discovered that a giant "monster," portrayed in
the illustration as an octopus (and there really are giant octo-
puses in Puget Sound), was slouching up onshore when the
tide was out, covering the clams and geoducks with the long
reach of its menacing body. Furtively, Crow slipped a sharp
rock under the monster's body, forcing it to move and expose
the food. The grateful people (along with Crow) feasted
convivially, side by side.

Wendell Berry often uses the word *convivial* to characterize our potential relationship with the wider earth, an apt and unusual word in this context. *Convivial* is an adjective implying a participatory liveliness; it is derived from the Latin *convivium*, a joining of *con*, "with," and *vivere*, "to live." Eric Partridge notes that *vivere* refers not just to humans but also to other creatures, and he points to the Latin word *convivia*, another word for "a banquet" but also "a fellow banqueter." The notion of conviviality thus unfolds into a joining of living creatures about a celebratory meal, a shared feast—but what a peculiar table this is. As humans, we have a unique role in determining the well-being of our more-than-human communities. Coexistence is complicated, but one thing is sure: we share the land in the broad Leopoldian sense, and so we share the food, water, and elbow room—the convivial sense of a common life. We cannot set the table by—or for—ourselves alone.

Most of us in urban and suburban places live, however unwittingly, in a multilayered *zoöpolis*—a wonderful term coined by geographer Jennifer Wolch. A zoöpolis is the place where the polis meets the zoo, an overlap of human and animal geographies. Most often, a zoöpolis is formed when humans build their homes on land that historically has belonged to nonhumans, or when we create landscapes in which particular species known as *synanthropes* ("with-humans") can prosper alongside us. Certain bird species are among the most visible and accessible native wild synanthropes, and without much effort most of us could look past the House Sparrows, pigeons, and starlings to find a native bird species other than a crow in our neighborhood—perhaps a robin, a finch, or a kind of jay. The zoöpolis may be a dumbed-down sort of place by wild ecosystemic standards, but it is likely to be far more vibrant than most of us imagine. While writing behind my study window today I have seen Steller's Jays, Northern Flickers, Black-capped Chickadees, Anna's Hummingbirds, starlings, and several crows. I have listened to the rustling of the squirrels that have insistently taken shelter in the high corner of our attic in spite of our best squirrel-torment regimen (involving mainly a broom handle pounded on the gutter). Looking up, I started at the sudden, unexpected sight of an adult Sharp-shinned Hawk perched on tall yellow legs right there on the crow wire. I didn't even have time to reach for my binoculars before it flew away, flat and quick. All of this in just twelve minutes or so. This year to date we have seen thirty-seven species of birds in or around our yard, including Turkey Vultures, Bald Eagles, Caspian Terns, Yellow Warblers, Townsend's Warblers, Hermit Thrushes, Western Tanagers, and Bushtits. It is a good number, but Jim and Marissa, my birder neighbors on the next block, have tallied fifty-seven species, which can only mean that in spite of my binocular toting and persistent household-nature note taking, I *still* have not been paying close enough attention. We have also seen raccoons (too bold and far too many; they like to dismantle my pond lilies and hunt my koi, and they wash their "hands" so earnestly in the little pool above the waterfall that I am half-inclined to leave them a bar of soap), possums, mounded evidence of at least one thriving mole, eight species of butterfly, and countless insects, arachnids, and isopods (terrestrial and subterrestrial), not to mention the slugs, snails, and earthworms that wend their way about my home both day and night. Right here in Seattle, just beyond my little yard and neighborhood (and sometimes intersecting with either or both, with or without my knowing), there are three species of mole (including the Pacific Northwest endemic shrew-mole), deer mice, house mice, and more rats than I want to think about, including wood rats, wharf rats (also called sewer rats), pack rats, Norway rats, and the wonderfully named *Rattus rattus* — the black rat. There are squirrels, both native (such as the Douglas Squirrel and the uncommon Northern Flying Squirrel, both requiring a modicum of forested habitat) and introduced (the common Eastern gray squirrel of parks, yards, and college campuses), rabbits (mainly introduced, including the Eastern cottontail, and nearly one hundred varieties of domestic rabbits and their hybrids), porcupines, spotted skunks, striped skunks, muskrats and nutria (near freshwater), Canada Geese, Mallards, several species of gull (don't call them "seagulls" — it is inaccurate and upsets the birders), Bald Eagles, Osprey, Red-tailed Hawks, bank-tower and bridge-nesting Peregrine Falcons, Barred Owls, Great Horned Owls, Western Screech Owls, one hundred other species of birds at various times throughout the migratory year, and also assorted frogs, toads, salamanders, snakes, turtles, and lizards. There are several species of bat, including the most common Little Brown Bat, though in my yard I have seen only the dead, crow-eaten one. There are, we know, coyotes; they sometimes venture beyond the parks that are their cobbled woodsy confines to eat the dog food left on back porches, or slow cats. In one of the larger wooded parks there is a pair of ravens some years, and here and there are tracts of forest that can support the large, red-crested Pileated Woodpecker. Occasionally I see them on the rotting utility pole that holds up my crow wire, the pole favored by the Northern Flicker, the most common urban woodpecker throughout the country. The suburbs surrounding Seattle and the watersheds that they depend upon are home to still more, and bigger, animals: black-tailed deer, elk, black bears, fox, bobcats, and cougars with spotted kits, and still more species of birds, rodents, bats, and everything else.

Seattle may be known for its gorgeous setting and its outdoor-minded inhabitants, but as a thriving zoöpolis it is not unique. Other urban and suburban centers are home to geographic variations of all of the above. They are inhabited by all manner of beings, all with their attendant variety of behaviors and habits. Though we seldom see, or even think about, most of these organisms, it is nevertheless true that with a bit of time, thought, effort, ingenuity, practice, and perhaps assistance from someone who knows about such things, we could observe almost all of them. And—with or without ingenuity and regardless of our inclination—we live among them, and they among us. It is highly likely that on this list of creatures, humans are the only ones with the capacity to give the question of how to graciously coexist some attention (assuming for the moment that the crows are not actually holding urban planning meetings, as they so often appear to be doing). It seems that allowing the zoöpolis to thrive falls to us.

How do we manage such a living? How do we set the interspecies table and navigate our place in this field of beings and the conflicts such a life necessarily entails? For landowners (as all home dwellers are, in a pared-back but still meaningful sense), it goes without saying that our own interests and those of the other species in our community will not be identical. Common animals such as crows, sparrows, pigeons, raccoons, and coyotes are frequently perceived as nuisances and even threats to humans. Urban wildlife biologist Russell Link, who authored the brilliant and comprehensive manual *Living with Wildlife in the Pacific Northwest* (which, despite its title, is useful throughout North America), writes that human/wild conflicts in urban and suburban places normally fall into one of three categories. An animal or group of animals might be considered destructive (to houses, structures, gardens, and so on); aggressive (a threat to people or pets); or a health risk (potentially passing diseases or parasites to people or pets). Crows, with their dive-bombing, raucous scolding, garbage thieving, garden eating, and perceived dirtiness, are regularly accused of all of these things.

Link notes that none of these conflict categories are the least bit straightforward. For one thing, the threat is very often imagined rather than actual, based on a mythologized or naive understanding of wildlife. Wild animals are often blamed for things they didn't in fact do (such as when a dog rather than a crow or raccoon knocks down the garbage can and spreads its contents). Neighbors may disagree about which animals should be tolerated, and about what tolerance means. Some people might feed and shelter more wildlife than their neighbors are comfortable with, sometimes inadvertently (such as when a wild-bird feeder also attracts rats, or an outdoor dog-food bowl invites raccoons), sometimes on purpose. (I recently noticed a rather shocking number of pigeons gathering regularly in the yard behind us. When I finally walked over to meet our new neighbor Lacey, she warmly took my hand and said, "Oh, you're the girl that worked for Audubon. *You'll* understand." She then showed me her impressive stash of semi-stale bread, which she tosses twice daily.) Some people misguidedly "tame" wild animals with food, and then these animals become nuisances in the neighborhood, overly comfortable around humans. Link emphasizes the animal's lack of guilt in the human sense. "When a conflict exists between humans and animals," he writes, "it is usually because the animal is only doing what it needs to do to survive. It is simply following its own instincts, and intends no harm or discomfort." Almost always, an understanding of wild animal behavior sheds light on the situation.

It is ironic that the conflicts are invariably framed from the human perspective, when it is typically human encroachment that has caused the problem, and it is most likely the wild animal that will ultimately suffer as a result. Nearly all of our urban planning frames the city as a home for humans and fails to account for the presence and needs of nonhuman animals. Even "sustainable city" efforts pay little attention to the needs of animals per se, focusing instead on issues of water purity, clean air, parks, and green space for the health, recreational, and aesthetic benefits they confer upon humans. As ill-conceived housing developments sprawl into areas that were very recently forested, the human/wild clashes become more complicated, sometimes involving displaced elk, black bears, or cougars that unwittingly wander back into their previous home range, where they are no longer welcome; such situations too often culminate in the death of the dislocated animal. In a recent Seattle incident, a young black bear somehow found itself in the very urban district near the University of Washington. In a reaction termed a "comedy" by the Seattle papers, the bear was surrounded by "wildlife enforcement officers" and a full-on SWAT team, and shot with tranquilizers and Tasers until it lay down and died.

Other conflicts are far less visible. As human habitation and commercial ventures encroach relentlessly upon limited green space, native vegetation for feeding, nesting, and shelter are depleted, while supplemental food for predators and aggressive species increases. Birds that might survive on the borders of urban landscapes with even a modicum of contiguous forest (such as the Song Sparrow, Downy Woodpecker, Western Tanager, and Brown Creeper) are replaced by even more starlings (which nest on buildings) and, of course, crows (which eat human refuse). I recall Jack Turner's lament in his challenging book *The Abstract Wild*: "We lost the wild bit by bit for ten thousand years and forgave each loss and then forgot." Most of the landscape modification in urban communities occurs outside of the typical resident's daily awareness and concern. We don't notice the gradual shift in species until one day we ask, "Where did all these crows come from?"

The historian and activist Thomas Berry believes it is humanity's "great work" to become a viable species on this changing earth. A species' viability is a measure of its evolutionary success and its ecological outlook. Ecologically, a species is said to be viable if it exists in appropriate numbers in the proper landscape, and if there is enough habitat to support sustainable numbers into the foreseeable future. For humans, whose continued success (at least population-wise) is not in question, viability becomes a different kind of issue. With our distinctive capacity to choose our lifestyles and consumption patterns, the notion of viability takes on, for us, another layer of meaning. For humans to be viable on a planet in ecological crisis, we must not only maintain balanced populations but do so in a way that allows our supporting habitat to thrive—that is, we must live respectfully, wisely, considerately, and graciously alongside the nonhuman community, or as Thomas Berry puts it, be "present to the earth in a mutually enhancing manner." This will mean a substantial rethinking of our role at the earthen table, allowing the grace of difference and diversity in our more-than-human communities to be granted weight and value. It will mean engaging a modern version of Aldo Leopold's land ethic, the foundation of which must be an expansive conception of our urban homes as *land* (again, *all things on, over, or in the earth*). It will mean thinking, sometimes, and as best we can, from the standpoint of a nonhuman animal. For this we are shockingly ill-equipped.

The following letter about backyard crows recently appeared in our neighborhood paper, the *West Seattle Herald*:

> Hitchcock where art thou? West Seattle is the place for your next horror film. All the joy of feeding birds and squirrels peanuts and wild birdseed is over. Bullies from the sky with sharp-as-a-tack radar swoop in five, 10, 15 at a time to carry off all my offerings. No random acts of kindness for others, not in my backyard anyway. These are big, menacing vultures. What can a bird feeder do?

I must shamefully admit that my immediate reaction utterly lacked compassion. "Idiot," I said out loud. I mean, honestly, the woman surrounds her house with grass, tosses about handfuls of peanuts and "wild birdseed" (whatever that means), then wonders why there are crows (an animal she seems not to recognize as a "wild bird")? She finds "joy" in feeding an invasive plague of bushy-tailed diurnal ratlike rodents yet has nothing but derision for a native corvid? And I can only wonder what "acts of kindness" she imagines a proper bird might proffer? But then I realize that I ought to be more understanding.

Obviously this woman loves animals—some of them, anyway—and she means well. People who feed birds normally do so because they think that putting out feeders is what people who love birds do. Bird feeding can be done well, but the enormous commercial birdseed and -feeder industry keeps it a secret that unless they are scrupulously cared for, feeders often invite disease, nonnative birds (such as starlings), and rats. Feeders may even interrupt natural migration patterns, as birds that would normally fly to Central or South America during the colder (typically foodless) seasons find an artificial source of abundant food and decide to stick around. These birds may succumb to the winter cold, or perhaps eventually contribute to the rearrangement of migration patterns with unforeseeable ecological consequences (the arguments for such a scenario remain largely anecdotal but are nevertheless plausible). Surely if this woman were better informed, she would engage her love for birds in a more ecologically viable manner. Armed with this bodhisattva-like mind-set, I revisit the letter but am disappointed to discover that I fare no better. "Idiot," I hear myself whisper (a bit more softly, at least).

In a flip side to this story, I was recently rambling along the tree-line trail above the water at Lincoln Park and passed a dead Pacific madrona whose branches were fairly dripping with crows. I am not normally disconcerted by crow gatherings, but these birds truly evoked the eerie schoolyard gathering scene in Hitchcock's *The Birds*. I stopped to look them over, reckoning that they were the family group whose nest had been in the big hawthorn tree by the ball field. An older man ahead of me on the trail noticed my interest. "Those are my friends," he told me. "Watch." He reached into the plastic grocery bag he was carrying, grasped a handful of something, and threw it into the air. It hit the ground and the crows descended. "Dog food," he responded to my inquiring glance. Better than white bread, at least. "I get it at Safeway, just five dollars for fifty pounds!" He continued up the trail. "Come along!" he yelled, and sure enough, the crows followed.

He was clearly a sweet man, and his is a harmless confusion, is it not? Kindly tossing kibble to the park birds and calling them friends? At our house we colloquially indulge such fuzzy language all the time. "There's a friend in the bathroom!" Claire reports, and I know she is announcing a newly discovered spider. "Off to visit your friends?" Tom asks, when I head out the door with binoculars and a notebook in search of crows. Equivocating on the word, we can be a friend to wildlife by planting trees, or restoring land, or moving dead animals off the road so the scavengers that come to eat them don't become roadkill themselves. Occasionally, when wild animals such as crows are removed from their own society at an early age, they become lively pets. But it is normally inaccurate to call wild animals friends.

Friends share a bond of *mutual* affection. I am not saying it is impossible for a human and a wild animal to be friends in this sense—I have heard stories about such relationships that seem to be true, and I sometimes imagine them for myself. But typically, though we may feel affection for wild animals, their feelings for us must be characterized by something different. Fear or indifference, normally. In our close urban quarters, and with birds as smart as crows, there often develops a tolerance based on familiarity (especially if we carry bags of dog food around). But if we are careful in our language, and in our perception, we will be wary about notions of friendship.

It is little wonder that we are confused about such things. As a culture, we have allowed the development of our natural intelligence to founder. Richard Louv has outlined the scope of "nature deficit disorder" for children in his book *Last Child in the Woods,* but the same issues plague us as adults—as models, mentors, parents, and teachers. If we are truly concerned about the development of children's natural intelligence, then we must tend just as urgently to our own. We have been offered no easy venue for learning the basic needs and habits of the wild animals that surround us. Not only were our science classes abstract—not specific to the organisms that characterize the biotic communities in which we live—but these very communities are, in themselves, of dubious natural character. Any landscape marked by human intrusion is, in ecological parlance, *disturbed,* and as a habitat-type, the urban landscape can only be called *highly disturbed.* The word *disturb* has a Latin root, *turbare,* which means "to agitate" or "to confuse," "to pour together," "to mix utterly." How fitting! Wild and domestic. Native and introduced. Rare and invasive. Pavement and pathway. Human and wild. The extraordinary and the commonplace. Crows, dogs, forest orchids, hothouse orchids, hummingbirds, parakeets, Republicans. All living together. All eating, breathing, drinking, spawning their seed, raising their young, leaping, crawling, questioning, thriving, just ever so barely getting by. No wonder most of us are mystified about our proper relationship to wild life, when our substrate itself is so thoroughly confounded. No wonder we are unprepared for this remarkable banquet. No wonder we close our eyes, toss birdseed, and hope for the best.

An administrator at my daughter's school whom I like very much told me that after her cat was eaten by a coyote, she was overcome for months with fear—fear that the coyote would "get" her children, or perhaps her cocker spaniel (a dog actually too big for a coyote). These concrete (though unfounded) worries lay alongside a more amorphous, unspecifiable dread. We have backed ourselves into a paradox—loving the idea of the wild from an aesthetic, recreational, and perhaps moral dimension, and particularly loving the idea that we have not eradicated all wild things. *There are still coyotes in the city? There are mountain lions in the hills? Yes!* We are pleased with ourselves at the thought of their presence; it reflects well on us—does it not?—that they are here. But nothing will eradicate such goodwill more quickly than the sighting of a cougar anywhere near a school-yard or, say, a backyard coyote eating Fluffy the cat. Regarding our incongruent feelings about the wildlife around our homes, Russell Link writes, "We want them and we don't want them, depending on what they are doing at any given moment."

Unawares, we have drawn a squiggly psychic line. Wild robins are pretty. No one minds robins. Or chickadees, of course, or the rest of the "garden" birds. But what about the others? What about all of the common wild animals that simply do not and will not stay neatly in place? What about raccoons? Or bats? What about coyotes? Coyotes are large and little understood, and they look a bit too much like wolves. What about the Sharp-shinned Hawk perched near the feeder we put out, hunting "our" birds? What about crows? So often these common urban animals are perceived to be just too—Too what? Too *wild*? What can that possibly mean? Here are the real questions that will determine our species' viability. We live alongside wild life. We choose whether our children will enjoy such privilege. Coexistence in the zoöpolis will sometimes involve a vague uneasiness. Can we come to live comfortably in this slight discomfort? Can we rejoice in its meaning?

Russell Link suggests that to live well in the zoöpolis, we humans are going to have to become more responsible for ourselves and, simultaneously, more tolerant of some encroachment, inconvenience, and damage from wild animals. In this light, I think of the modern crows among us, continuing to "set the table," reminding us how to live side by side. Not because they are good at it themselves, but because they live so thoroughly among us, a constant announcement of ever-present wild life. Living daily alongside crows, I remember to check the lid on the garbage can, to refrain from observing too closely the warbler's nest in the backyard vine maple lest I draw a predator's attention, to put a net over the koi pond at night. I'm reminded that when the raccoon does get a fish, just as when raccoons killed two of our backyard chickens, it's my own dumb fault. I am reminded to step outside after dusk, no matter how chill the air, to see if I might hear an owl or a nighthawk or finally find a bat, to keep renewing a hopeful interest in the wild things around my home. I'm reminded to fight like hell for the green space that will allow a range of species to flourish, not just the synanthropes but the birds that can live near cities as long as areas of contiguous forest are conserved or restored. I am reminded to provide shelter, if I can, for species that might be induced to live with me in this "disturbed system" even though their natural homes have been removed by habitat loss or taken over by more aggressive species. For us this means a Violet-green Swallow box under the eaves, and the still-uninhabited bat box on the other side of the house (a female flicker has taken up roosting there as the weather cools). I'm reminded to keep replacing the grass with native plants and shrubs that flourish in local conditions while providing natural food and cover for wild birds (the single best way to limit numbers of dominant birds such as crows and starlings that thrive on the confluence of concrete and traditional "yard"). I'm reminded to tend our small vegetable garden with my daughter, so we will all remember where food really comes from and what our bodies, turned to light work, are good for. I'm reminded to keep my head on straight. I'm reminded when I wake up in the morning, even if the dawn chorus is nothing but the "Caw! Caw!" of the neighborhood crows, that I must renew my delight and effort in this tangled banquet. I am reminded daily, by this smart, endlessly wonderful, shining bird I have come to know, but not quite love, to do all I possibly can to keep the earth from degenerating into a planet full of nothing but crows.

Nine

DYING

Crows of Death and Life

...Who is stronger than death?
Me, evidently.
Pass, Crow.

— TED HUGHES

One morning, I opened the curtains to survey the damage wrought by the previous night's windstorm. Other than a few scattered branches and overturned trash cans, all seemed well except for the—

And before I could even finish noticing that a junco was lying dead in the grass, a crow swooped in next to the smaller bird and picked it up handily in her bill. She walked to the sidewalk and tucked the bird neatly under her feet, as crows do, enjoying the traction that a sturdy substrate allows as they hold food down with their toes and pull it apart with their bills.

I called Claire. We watch crows nearly every day, but this seemed a particularly potent way to start the morning, with the ecological imperatives of life and death unfolding before our eyes. The crow was plucking wildly—little bits of feather and fluff flew north, the way the wind was blowing. Morsels of flesh and sinew were torn off and consumed between bouts of continued feather removal. "So that bird is really"—Claire paused, seeking the mot juste—"dead." The pronouncement was conferred with seeming finality and scientific objectivity. But then, in a moment of glorious hope that she tried to disguise, she asked, "Isn't it?" So there it was: death's nearness and necessity, and our simultaneous acceptance of and ambivalence toward nature's dearest lesson, all before the milk was even poured over our oatmeal.

In our everyday lives, we see remarkably little evidence in support of the obvious fact that all living things die. Animals nearing death tend to be secretive, returning their bodies to earth in quiet, unseen ways. Even people who spend a great deal of time in wilder places wonder from time to time where all the dead animals are. In cities and suburbs this is no less true, though the decomposition process, which proceeds so beautifully upon soil, is hampered by the frequent occurrence of concrete, and the suddenness of death-by-auto keeps many animals from hiding away at their passing. But it is for these very reasons that city living can, if we let it, bring us just as close to a necessary awareness of the hidden deaths that turn the cycles of life as a walk in a pristine forest would—and perhaps even closer.

In wilder places, we may chance upon the body of a larger animal—a white-tailed deer, a Roosevelt elk, perhaps a black bear—in any possible stage of decomposition. We hardly ever see a dead bird, though of course they are there. And in these wilderness places, we tend to view death in terms of a romanticized ecological harmony. "It is part of nature," we recite blandly to our children, pleased with ourselves for confronting such bold lessons with a placid wisdom. All of the bodies, all of the deaths, seen and unseen, are gathered under the umbrella of natural earthly processes, occasionally tugging at our sentimental human hearts, but clearly not tragic. And the deaths of wild animals are equal—that is to say, while the elk's corpse might give us greater pause, it is not *sadder* than the death of the Townsend's vole or the Winter Wren. It is not properly sad at all, wrapped in the necessary dynamism of nature's cycles. This we know.

How odd, then, that once we slip off our Gore-Tex–lined boots and return to our homes in the urbs or the suburbs or the exurbs, our reaction to dead animals suddenly varies according to the manner of beast. Dead pets are tragic, of course (some child loved them). Dead robins are sad (such a beautiful "part of nature"). Dead rats are gross (and remind us that rats are among us, which we prefer not to acknowledge). Dead possums are unfortunate (but what do they expect, plodding so myopically across the street in the dark?). And dead crows are—Well, who really cares about dead crows? Dead crows are dead crows. We don't see many of them, though we have all seen at least one—probably in the late summer, when the corpses of naive young crows dot the streets. But in death, crows seem to be eminently ignorable. Neither reviled enough to be horrific nor beautiful enough to be lamented, they are, perhaps, one of the most perfectly ignored dead animals in the world. This is a curious turn, given that crows are associated so closely in the human psyche with death, our darkest shadow-fear—and not without good reason. In spite of their own overlooked deaths, crows lie at the heart of nature's most difficult and urgent lesson in the cultivation of our own ecological maturity: the necessity of keeping death ever before us.

Various animals are twined, in our minds, with the idea of death. There are those that can kill us, such as grizzly bears, mountain lions, and some snakes. There are those we think of as killing humans but that hardly ever do, such as wolves. There are those that scavenge already-dead animals, such as vultures, condors, ravens, and crows. Much more than the land-dwelling carnivores, it is these birds and their wings, bearing a simultaneous connection to earth and heaven, that have lent themselves so effortlessly to millennia of crosscultural art, myth, and symbol surrounding death. The vultures of Egyptian art and hieroglyphics come easily to mind. But of all the animals that we associate with death — whether through science, art, or subconscious machination — crows are the only one that most modern humans are likely to encounter regularly, even daily, making them a potentially compelling guide, both symbolically and biologically, through the indeterminate realm between life and death.

The corvid family predates Homo sapiens on earth by several million years. This means that crows spent a long evolutionary history perfecting their ecological role as scavengers millennia before humans began dying. When humans did appear, and especially when they took to dying in convenient congregations, the crows were ready. Even thousands of years ago, warriors knew that it was their potential destiny to be eaten by crows, and from the Renaissance wars of Europe

to the American Civil War, crows were known to follow sol-
diers to battle, wait in the trees, and feed upon the dead.

In medieval Europe, the bubonic plague spread with
merciless efficiency across the continent, killing twenty-five
million people of all ages and classes, one-third of Europe's
population within five years. Whole families were swiftly
stricken, and their neighbors would learn of their deaths
only when the stench reached their windows. Bodies were
dragged out of houses and left lying before the doors or
sometimes piled onto makeshift biers. Rats are the animal
most famously linked with the plague, serving as a vector for
the virus between fleas and humans, but at the time, no one
understood the source of the plague, and the animals most
keenly associated with the Black Death (so called in England
because of the dark blotches that formed on the skin of the
afflicted) were the crows and ravens that scavenged the bodies lying uncovered in the streets, beginning, horribly, with
the eyeballs. To fix the image, the few doctors willing to visit
the ill wore steel masks with large screened eye holes and a
protruding "beak" filled with perfume or spices to offset the
stench of decaying bodies. They looked just like giant crows.

The great London fire of 1666 cemented a centuries-long
hatred of crows. Ravens and crows descended with such
zeal upon the charred victims that the grieving survivors
appealed to King Charles II, begging him to exterminate the
birds, a task he oversaw with vigor. Nests were decimated
and bounties paid on the skins of crows and ravens.

For cultures with a deeply religious, cultural, or psychological attachment to an intact body, crows' pecking of

human corpses was particularly horrific. For us moderns, the notion of being eaten by a crow under any circumstances seems a remote possibility. Still, the very thought of being bodily consumed represents a primal fear, one with which most of us can viscerally identify. It is little wonder that crows are portrayed in many European superstitions as avatars of death.

Other cultural associations between crows and death are more balanced, welcoming crows as liaisons between worlds. The connection was made most plain in Tibet where, until the 1950s, "sky burials" were still common. The bodies of loved ones were ceremoniously carved into small pieces and placed on outdoor altars for crows, ravens, and other avian scavengers who literally carried the bodies into the next life. In her lovely book *Ravensong,* Catherine Feher-Elston recounts the philosophy and legend of Native American plains groups, many of whom saw in the crow a mediator between the visible world of the earth and the invisible world of the spirit-dead. The birds could communicate with the dead, and in so doing help living humans to navigate their lives with greater wisdom. In some myths, crows appear as teachers, showing humans how to traverse the complexities of the dying process. A thirteenth-century commentary on the Talmud has a crow directing the first human funeral. Observing that Adam and Eve had no sense of what to do with the body of their dead son Abel, the crow killed one of his own companions and buried it by way of example, while the skins-clad couple watched.

It is my belief that many of these images from the human

cultural history, captured in collective memory, myth, and art, partly color and construct our association of crows with death. But only in part. No one who lives in any kind of proximity to crows will get far on in years without seeing a crow eating a road-killed squirrel, rat, or other hapless beast. And so the historical and mythological associations are made perfectly plain for present-day eyes. Crows eat dead things, and often we get to watch them.

My *get to* here might seem sarcastic, but it is not meant to be. Most modern humans, if we pay any kind of attention at all, are privy to the basic cycles of nature. We can, after all, see trees turn dormant in the winter and flower in the spring, observe the phases of the moon, and come to know the migratory patterns of local birds. And yet the essential turning, the moment of death, the subsequent decay and return to earth, the nourishment that such turnings bring to new lives — all of this is very often beyond our awareness, no matter how well we watch. Nearly all wild creatures do their dying out of public view, hiding themselves away to pass in secret, and in solitude. Only a few very social animals, such as crows, sometimes gather at the death of one in their family group. But in the places that humans and animals intersect most frequently — urban and suburban neighborhoods where people do lots of driving — we are afforded an uncommonly regular view of the wild's most compulsory, most intimate moment. We sometimes accidentally kill animals ourselves or see them in the road where others have not managed to miss them. Not in favor of having dead things in front of our houses, we efficiently whisk them away. But some of the roadkills fall through the cracks, not being close enough to a particular doorstep for anyone to claim them. These animals are left, and while they are still fresh, crows eat them.

It is fascinating to watch. While eating something as complicated as another animal, crows deftly use their feet as braces, holding the food secure while tearing at it with their dexterous bills. Sinewy muscle tissue is tough, and crows lean hard into their work. Their feet work almost as hands sometimes, grasping, pulling, twisting, arranging. Crows are remarkably watchful over their food. If you approach a crow in the midst of eating a fresh squirrel, it will be decidedly reluctant to leave, and though it will become nervous in the extreme, it will hold its mark a fair bit longer than if you just walked up to it while it was hanging out on the grass. (Because of this, we need to be particularly careful when driving toward crows that are eating in the road; while they would normally fly easily out of the way, they are more prone to miscalculation when absorbed in such meals. "They always move," drivers invariably proclaim when approaching a crow in the road, when the actual truth is that they usually move. *Usually* is a potent qualifier—in the slender margin between *usually* and *always* lies an untold number of dead crows.)

Anyone with basic ecological knowledge, or even a measure of common sense, knows that no matter how creepy it might seem, crows, as wild urban scavengers, are engaged in a remarkable, multilayered service: feeding themselves; allowing a dead animal the rightful honor of passing into the ecosystemic cycles rather than being squished into Velveetaoblivion; and removing animal flesh that would otherwise putrefy in our streets. And no matter how romantically we humans tend to wax about the harmonious beauty of nature's cycles, very few remember, in the case of crows, to give a nod of gratitude. Our crow nods are very often of a completely different sort.

"Crows are mean," my friend Sheila reported to me with biblical authority. I was sure I knew why she said so — the same reason so many say the same thing. "You've been dive-bombed by a crow?" I inquired. "Yes, and I wasn't even doing anything. Just walking along, minding my own business." I suggested that perhaps while she didn't *know* she was doing anything, she was probably walking past a tree in which the crow had a nest, maybe with eggs or freshly born young. Normally, this is the only case in which crows will actually swoop a person, and in this context it is admittedly not uncommon, particularly if the crows have been made to feel vulnerable — say, if another human, especially one wearing the same color as Sheila on that particular day, or having the same hairstyle or shape of glasses, has been loud or bothersome or threatening in the presence of the nest. But the crow's reaction is typically misunderstood, and it spurs the most common crow misconception — that crows are not only bold but somehow *mean-spiritedly* bold.

Crows are intelligent, yes, but it remains an error to confer a complex, nuanced emotion such as malice upon a bird, a feeling they do not, and probably cannot, possess. Crows are not even bold in the normal sense — that is, not courageous or fearless or defiant. Crow swooping is, if we can see it for a moment from the perspective of the crow, an act of necessity, of protection, and of wondrously careful parenting. It reflects the particular frailty of the crow's nest, being too big to hide, and having large, dark parent birds whose comings and goings, unlike those of most other songbird parents, can scarcely be kept secret. And the crows' alarm is not without reason. Newly hatched crows rest in their comfortable nest, mud and sticks on the outside but lined with moss and feathers and other soft things. They know nothing of the fact that this is their most vulnerable life's moment, the time when crow mortality is at its peak.

Here are some of the ways that young crows die: the eggs may fail to hatch (they are infertile or the embryos die within the egg or the eggs are destroyed or eaten by predators); the nest may be blown from the tree; nestlings may die from exposure in inclement weather; they may be fatally weakened by body parasites, either internal or external; they may succumb to starvation or to predation by raccoons, Great Horned Owls, Cooper's Hawks, or Red-tailed or Red-shouldered Hawks (all raptors are considered by crows to be potential threats, which is why we commonly observe crows boisterously mobbing any hawk or owl they see); or, naive after fledging, young crows may be approached and killed by people, cars, and cats.

Adult crows, too, are as vulnerable as any other being that, like us, is made of flesh, blood, and bone. They may be attacked while sleeping by nocturnal predators such as owls or raccoons. They may die from disease or starvation. They may be electrocuted as they perch on utility wires, or be hit by a car. They are susceptible to blood parasites, to bacterial infection from avian cholera, to lung tumors, to *Aspergillus* fungal infection, and to rabies contracted by scavenging rabid dead vertebrates. And now they are also dying from West Nile virus, which has, after a single dead crow in New York's Central Park tested positive for the disease in 1999, spread across the continent and killed hundreds of thousands of crows, devastating several local populations.

The crow diet is, in a backward way, another source of the species' vulnerability. Most animals have a dedicated food source. Crows, for the most part, do not—they are omnivores, taking whatever comes. This seems like a happy fate for a bird, feasting daily upon the smorgasbord of life. And it is true that most crows in the past century have adapted well to changes in North America. With their fondness for corn, the proliferation of an agrarian lifestyle served them well; crow populations grew and spread. As urban centers sprouted with their attendant suburbs, the crows' plastic diet allowed them to thrive, even as other avian species were forced to retreat. Still, life as an omnivore can prove an onerous prospect, and in some cases it is more difficult than being a crossbill, say, tweezing seeds out of cones all day, knowing what it must do and where it must do it. A crow does not know what the day's food will be. A meal must be sought out, wrung from its place, and perhaps defended. Scavenged animals are just one element of the crow's omnivorous diet. Crows may also consume berries, seeds, nuts, lizards, frogs, snakes, worms, eggs, spiders, and insects. Crows are attracted to the suburbs in part for the fresh, nutritious roadkill available, including

possums, raccoons, squirrels, and cats. In their recent evolutionary history, urban crows have come to enjoy donuts,
bagels, hamburgers, shredded wheat, tuna sandwiches,
chocolate chip cookies, and pizza. Dead animals are eaten
for necessary protein, vitamins, minerals, and—as the luck
and beauty of ecological balance would have it—for us (*us*
being all of the creatures that happen not to be crows), eating
the dead things off our streets before they become stenching,
maggoty piles of decomposing flesh.

Crows are normally believed to be notorious nest robbers,
consuming both the eggs and nestlings of smaller songbirds,
but John Marzluff's research suggests the need for a nuanced
reading of this prevalent crow mythology. In extensive studies involving artificial ground nests, shrub nests, and canopy
nests, Marzluff found no positive relationship between crow
abundance and the rate of predation. Crows *do* prey on nests,
he concluded, but they are just one of nearly twenty potential
nest predators, including large and small mammals, owls,
and hawks. In neighborhoods, jays (also corvids) are probably much more active nest predators than crows. The most
common nestlings taken by crows are robins, and though
we may feel some sympathy for the individual robins, as a
species they are in no ecological danger. I'm no crow apolo-
gist, but in this case the evidence seems to show that crows
have been given a disproportionate heap of the blame for a
practice that is carried out by many animals—and abetted
by human-caused habitat change, which makes forest birds
more accessible to all predators.

If crows appear menacingly bold, we do well to remember that they have ample reason. They are small creatures of flesh, finding food and raising young in a bustling, threatening landscape of larger, dangerous mammals, many of whom hate crows and drive SUVs. We share with crows an interconnected frailty, an utter dependence on the same wonderful, chaotic nature that metes out our life, our breath, our death, and eventually swallows every one of us whole.

Our fear of crows as dive-bombing harbingers of death has been played out in an oft-misguided revenge upon the birds themselves. In the modern psyche, a crow's life seems to be worth less than nearly any other wild animal's. Crows are one of the very few native wild birds that hunters across the country can kill in open seasons with no bag limits. Their evening roosts, perceived as too loud, too dirty, or just too creepy, are often dispersed by explosions, poisons, or outright shooting. While most other killing of animals in the name of flock or farm protection requires a permit, several agricultural states offer an exemption that allows farmers to kill crows at will. Even some pilgrims to Mecca may be excused from the journey's prohibition on killing to dispatch crows.

While most birds seem to have little awareness of death, crows join the animals we consider to be most intelligent, those with complex social groups, such as dolphins, elephants, and various primates, in a more nuanced response to the death of their kind. It seems that crows are initially alarmed by the death of another crow, boisterously calling and often gathering in a swooping crowd. It is possible that this is an alert to other crows of the potential for danger

associated with the area. But after the initial clamor, a stillness often settles around a dead crow's body. Several crows,
possibly among the dead bird's extended family of parents,
siblings, and cousins, sometimes cluster about the crow in
perfect silence, seemingly absorbed in contemplation before
the dead bird. The scene is affecting, and I have heard stories from several people who have witnessed such gatherings. These "crow funerals" have yet to be studied in any
kind of academic way, and it is difficult to even imagine what
that might mean. Perhaps this indeterminate place between
story and science is where these rites are most properly kept.
"I usually don't pay attention to crows at all," Gita, a young
metro-hip architect, told me, "but I was out jogging, and
these crows were *so quiet,* so amazingly still. When I saw
the dead crow on the ground under the branch they perched
on, I was just amazed. I lingered for several minutes. It was
beautiful. It changed my whole day."

Such awareness can surely change our days, but it can
also change our ways, our habit of being in relation to the
changing earth and its array of species. In reminding us
of the nearness and necessity of death, crows emerge again
as a kind of guide, showing us not only how to watch but
also what to watch for. In this, they join an impressive lineage of philosophers and spiritual thinkers. In chapter 4
of his sixth-century Rule for monastics, Saint Benedict
exhorted a person striving for spiritual maturity to "keep
death ever before you." His *mortem cotidie ante oculos sus-
pectam habere* might be more literally translated as "keep
death always suspect before your eyes." That is, more than

making death an object of meditation, live every moment with the knowing suspicion that one's own death could come at any time, which of course is true. It seems that Benedict did not mean for such an awareness to serve as a particular deterrent to vice, but rather as an impetus for reordering one's life, as Terrence Kardong writes in his exhaustive study of Benedict's Rule, to retrain "our absorption in fleeting, transitory affairs." It may not be coincidental that Benedict wrote the Rule after having his life saved by the bread-foiling crow.

Others have gone much further in recommending meditation upon one's death as a potent tool for properly orienting one's life. In the *Satipatthana Sutta,* the Buddhist Sutra on the Four Establishments of Mindfulness, the historical Buddha gives a series of lessons on stabilizing the mind and body as preparation for insight into the nature of being. One of the central exercises is titled "Body as Impermanent," a guided visualization to aid meditation on the transitory, ever-decomposing nature of the earthly body. There are nine stages of contemplation in the exercise, and the practitioner is invited to enter into deep meditation upon each, visualizing the stage in the mind's eye and allowing the knowledge thus attained to penetrate viscerally before progressing to the next stage. The nine contemplations are these:

1. The corpse is bloated, blue, and festering.
2. The corpse is crawling with insects and worms. *Crows,* hawks, vultures, and wolves are tearing it apart to eat.

3. All that is left is a skeleton with some flesh and blood still clinging to it.
4. All that is left is a skeleton with some blood stains.
5. All that is left is a skeleton with no more blood stains.
6. All that is left is a collection of scattered bones — here an arm, here a shin, here a skull, and so forth.
7. All that is left is a collection of bleached bones.
8. All that is left is a collection of dried bones.
9. The bones have decomposed, and only a pile of dust is left.

"When you first read this, you may feel that this is not a pleasant meditation," Vietnamese Buddhist monk and peace activist Thich Nhat Hanh writes in his commentary on the sutra without, I think, meaning to be wry. He continues:

> The effect of this practice can be very great. It can be liberating and can bring us much peace and joy. The practitioner observes mindfully in order to see the corpse at each of these stages and to see that it is inevitable that his or her own body will pass through the same stages.... Its intention is not to make us weary of life, but to help us see how precious life is; not to make us pessimistic, but to help us see the impermanent nature of life, so that we do not waste our life.

Nhat Hanh notes that such meditations were made more concrete in former times by the practice of actually sitting in cemeteries where corpses were, according to cultural custom, not buried, but left to decompose in the open. We should not be surprised, by now, to see crows turn up directly in the second contemplation. In fact, lacking the special circumstances of ancient monks in open cemeteries, we might look to scavenging crows to give us a rare glimpse into the stages outlined in the sutra.

Strikingly similar is an exhortation by the medieval abbot Arnulph of Boheries, who wrote in his *Mirror for Monks* that "assiduous reflection on death is the highest philosophy."

> If spiritual laziness does get hold, one should cure oneself of it by making a meditation about the stone slab on which the dead are washed. One should remind oneself how corpses on the way to burial are handled there, how they are turned face upwards and face downwards, how the head hangs, the arms are limp, the thighs cold, the legs lie stiff; how the corpse is clothed and sewn up, how it is carried to the grave, left in the tomb, covered with earth, how it is devoured by worms and rots away like a stinking sack.

While recognizing that the imagery is perhaps a bit more graphic than current sensibilities typically favor, the Australian Cistercian monk Michael Casey observes that Arnulph's point remains entirely modern. We are all going to die — how would we live if we knew our death was imminent, and why on earth do we not already live that way? "Today is the day when infinite possibilities remain open before us," Casey writes, "if only we can shake off our torpor and reimagine a different future." And this, I strongly believe, is one of the reasons that crows, the one animal in our everyday life that lingers in full view over corpses in our streets, unsettle us in ways we cannot quite speak—as *shakers-off of torpor*. The steady, languid inertia of torpor is so much pleasanter—is it not?—than any kind of shaking. And this is the very same reason that crows are so entirely relevant to our place on a changing earth, to "reimagining a different future." They bring us into direct contact with the utterly essential, with what we prefer to avoid, with what the corporate-driven individual consumerism that runs more rampant now than ever in history contrives to hide, with the lesson we most dearly need to comprehend: that we are all nearly dead. That in light of that fact, just perhaps, our relentless, frenzied, earth-killing, over-outfitting of our temporal bodies and homes is the tiniest tad misguided. What was this body again? Oh yes, that heap of blue flesh lying on the soil, being picked at by the crows. As we lay up our treasures for a short moment on earth, the crows watch us, reaping what's given them: our shatteringly abundant refuse, the animals we failed to see and so ran over.

Off to visit my parents the other day, I drove the I-5 corridor from Seattle to Olympia. Someone driving a Hummer, a giant, golden H2, passed me on the highway, and I laughed out loud. Immediately, I realized that this was an environmentally inappropriate response. What would have been more proper? I recall watching a novelist who was exploring the intersection between spirituality and the environment being interviewed by Bill Moyers. "When I see someone driving a Hummer, I feel like vomiting," she said, with good reason. But I just can't quite match the sentiment. I mean, yes, clearly Hummers are an absolute blight and obscene in all respects—a monstrous, guzzling, polluting vehicle with an overt connection to militarization and a war mentality. But people who choose to drive Hummers are so far removed from the discussion of how to live appropriately in relation to the natural world that they are not worth even attempting to engage. Not worth our worry. We have to just let them go, at least for now. Really, let them go drive their Hummers. They are mercifully few, and their impact is relatively light.

Who is really sealing the fate of the earth? Who is walking the line that will determine whether humans may become the viable species we need to be in order for evolutionary processes to continue with beauty and meaning? Who is walking, actually, just the wrong side of this line? Me. Me and the millions like me who know how potent this earthly moment is, who know just what we must do, how radically we must act, who vomit over giant cars, who recycle and compost and buy organic fruit and turn down our thermostats, and yet who fail, out of convenience, or hurry, or compromise, or laziness, or gluttony, or a lack of heart, or a love of stuff, to act as fully and fanatically and creatively and joyously as we must, over and over again. The resolve we know we ought to seek cannot come from the lists that are suddenly gracing the covers of glossy magazines—everything from *Sierra* to *Elle*—outlining the "30 Things YOU Can Do to Stop Climate Change," lists we stick on our refrigerators, doing whatever we can accomplish most easily for a few weeks until we forget.

The kind of resolve that leads to a profoundly changed habit of being rises out of knowledge, out of elegant intimacy based in awareness of the more-than-human world—observation that teaches us, through the habits of birds, or the sleep of spiders, or the hiding places of mushrooms and snakes, or the dying of stars, or the tending of seeds, or whatever our chosen, interconnected love might be, that in the end (and long before), we are subject to the ecological dynamics of the earth, they are not subject to us. This is not a cynical understanding. It is gorgeous, reassuring, intimate, and holy. Three crows fly over, land on their leafless branch, and ignore me. Portents of death? I try to see them as they are, as portents of nothing but themselves, swirling like all of us in our beautiful, tangled, transitory lives. I blink, look at them straight, and try once more to shake loose the torpor.

Ten

FLYING

Wings, Reality, Hope

All that is wild, is winged.

— Jay Griffiths

This morning I rose early and went out walking while my sweeties were still in bed. I thought it might be a bit early for crows, but I did see two of them, leaping from a branch into the very windy air, where they flew upward, then gathered their wings in closely to swoop down. They repeated the arc over and over, in what seemed to be a game — pure windswept enjoyment. Eventually they shook their wings out and headed for the big fir a few blocks north. Like most birds, crows fly for practical reasons — to look for food, to get from the place they are to the place they want to go. But unlike most birds, crows also appear to fly for reasons that defy scientific explanation, though to us it seems obvious. They fly for fun. Any windy day will fling crows into the air like leaves, diving, wheeling, rising, tumbling. I see them, and think that if I were a bird, I would want to fly like a crow — with enough of a brain to love it. It might even make it worth it having to eat dead city rats if I could fly like that.

Bird flight carries an easy symbolism: the bearing of flesh heavenward. We look up, craning and yearning. Watching a bird in flight, we think of freedom, of creativity, of speed, of spring. We feel the lifting of our minds, the release of our thoughts, the flights of our fancy. We think of magical beings — dragons, fairies. We think of the rhythms of life and nature as the birds gather and disperse and migrate, morning, evening, spring, fall. Sometimes we just think of how pretty birds look flying, and how amazing it all is. Here are creatures with feet that touch the earth, as ours do, but look what they can do! We think of possibility.

At home, no one but Delilah is awake. Typical. We hunch happily over our cat food and coffee, and I spread out the *New York Times,* wherein I am greeted with fresh statistics on global climate change. Mark Serreze of the National Snow and Ice Data Center at the University of Colorado estimates that the Arctic Ocean will be completely ice-free in summer by 2030, much sooner than previously predicted, even by those who have been working to warn us of the effects of global climate change. Just a few years ago, Serreze says, he would have made a more conservative estimate—perhaps 2070 or 2100—but an amalgamation of evidence now indicates a more rapid warming, with its attendant consequences. Even a much less significant loss of 30 or 40 percent would have a devastating effect upon ice-dependent creatures such as walruses, ringed seals, ribbon seals, and polar bears, and species such as gray whales will decline as the crustaceans they feed upon, which also rely on ice, disappear. Horrific feedback loops are also being unleashed as white ice morphs into blue water, which absorbs more sunlight and warms even faster. No one has cataloged—possibly no one even can catalog—the far-reaching ecological devastation, that this melting will bring, touching thousands of species, millions of individuals, and the foundations of evolutionary processes. The year 2030. My daughter will be just thirty-one years old.

Seattle-area scientists with the National Oceanic and Atmospheric Administration's Pacific Marine Environmental Laboratory recently published a study in *Geophysics Research Letters* that echoes the warning of Serreze, emphasizing the fact that greenhouse gases linger in the atmosphere for up to five decades. This means that no matter how dramatically we slash emissions from cars and industry, the Arctic melting and other effects of radical climate change will intensify. "Have you looked into the eyes of a climate scientist recently?" Michael Pollan asks in a recent essay. "They look really scared."

Assuming they are not wiped out by West Nile virus, crows are likely to fare well in the coming ecological scenario. The crows of Tanzania offer a glimpse into the likely relationship between crows and a changing earth. In 1890, British officials introduced the House Crow to East and South Africa, where it rapidly naturalized. There are now between three hundred thousand and half a million House Crows in Tanzania's capital city, Dar es Salaam. My family visited Tanzania as I was finishing this book, and we watched disconcertedly as the crows drove native shorebirds from the few natural refuges, and then as they darkened the skies in great clouds of cawing blackness at dusk. The people hate them. Though it was assumed that upon introduction they would function as scavengers, the large corvids set to work eating corn, groundnuts, pulses, pawpaw, and mangoes. In rural areas, crows pull maize seedlings from the ground, and also eat corn right off the standing cob. I think of the crow fledglings pulling up my carrot seedlings; the luxury I had in enjoying their antics and then shopping at an upscale farmer's market is not shared by the rural poor in Tanzania. Houses are necessarily open in much of Africa for airflow against the heat, and the House Crows readily enter them, pull lids off sugar and grain containers and eat the contents, break and eat eggs, and sometimes steal small treasures—jewelry, toys, and even pets. They pillage the nests of native birds and devour native amphibians, all of which are already vulnerable in this ecologically degraded deforested country. The government of Tanzania has appealed to the UN for help in eradicating crows, but unless issues of human household garbage and the large, open landfills that spot the city are also addressed, killing crows won't help. They will return in whatever number the ecosystem—even if it is an urban ecosystem—can support. It is a topsy-turvy scenario in which wild birds have been made, by gross human error, purveyors of ecological destruction rather than members of ecological community. It is also a potential future for all human-crow relations as global warming continues apace, geographical aridity becomes more widespread, small native animals are struggling and unprotected, the rural poor are hungrier than ever, and crows survive with hardly a blink.

I look once more at the new climate change predictions that grace the paper. My winged reveries among the morning crows suddenly strike me as both frivolous and irrelevant. It is all just too overwhelming. I try to imagine what hope would look like in such a scenario, hope that bears any semblance of intelligence. There isn't any, I decide. There is no sensible hope. Despondently (and a little more painfully than intended) I plunk my head down on the breakfast table, just as Claire bounds down the stairs, resplendent in ballerina pajamas and pink-flushed morning face. "Mommy," she deadpans, "your hair is in the milk."

Certainly it is difficult not to be cynical. Despite Al Gore, Leonardo DiCaprio airlifted to the Arctic in shiny new winter boots on the cover of *Vanity Fair,* and footage of drowning polar bears on *Oprah,* the pace of our ecological destruction has never been so quick, so forceful, so unabashed. There have never been so many species threatened with extinction. We have the voices of science, poetry, literature, celebrity, we have the beauty of the earth itself, and what do we come up with as a model of ecological living? Two-hundred-dollar recycled designer jeans and a hybrid Lexus—a more *efficient* conquering of the earth. It was 1949 when Aldo Leopold wrote, "In our attempt to make conservation easy, we have made it trivial." He had no idea.

Claire crawls into my lap, and I think of the things I so often repeat to her. *It is a graced moment. You can be a blessing upon the earth or a burden.* She picks up a napkin and wipes one of my dairy-soaked locks. "You're sad," she says, "because you'll miss me while you're gone."

Two or three times a year, I travel four hours south to Mt. Angel, in Oregon's beautiful Willamette Valley, and stay at the Benedictine Abbey there, on the hill above the little town. Sometimes I make a working retreat, taking advantage of the time away from my daily routine at home to immerse myself in the rhythm of the monastic day—following the bells that call the monks and all who care to join them to the chapel several times a day from dawn until night to sing the liturgy of the hours, and falling into bouts of concentrated writing between bells. Sometimes I leave my laptop at home, and the only nod to official work is an ever-ready notebook and pencil in my pocket. Always I take long walks and watch the crows that gather in the surrounding agricultural landscape, the crows that dress exactly like the monks, all in black.

Today I am packing to go to the monastery for nearly a week, and Claire is right, I will miss her. Though I want her to know the value in a mother taking time for her own creative and interior life, I always regret leaving her, even for a few days, and in my current mood, this clinginess runs deeper than usual.

After some cereal, we go upstairs to ready Claire for school, and looking out my study window, I spot Charlotte perched on the crow wire, my bathtub crow with one broken leg. I recognize Charlotte right away by the way she roosts, resting her belly on the wire instead of standing up straight, as crows normally do. Her leg never healed properly, and it splays to the side when she feeds on the ground. I've been keeping an eye on her for months now, watching as she struggled along as a fledgling on the neighborhood sidewalks, then as a fully grown (if a bit scrawny) first-year bird, miraculously dodging cats, raccoons, and migrating Cooper's Hawks.

Injured crows very often survive where birds of other species would perish. Their terrific intelligence and omnivorous diet allow a behavioral range unavailable to most birds. Where an injured warbler would huddle and starve, an injured crow can mix and scratch. In a park setting, where crows are accustomed to people, I have noticed that injured crows will more closely approach a person tossing bits of food than a healthy crow typically does. With a permanent injury — crumpled foot or one blind eye, for example — the already-difficult crow life is even harder. These birds make do. Whenever a person tells me he or she has been feeding a crow on the back porch, it almost always turns out that the bird is injured. Even crows with broken, hanging wings whose open injuries have healed but whose broken bones were never set, so they cannot fly, sometimes survive for a time. They stake out a territory on the ground and scavenge and beg. They may not have a long life, but most avian species couldn't pull off any semblance of such an existence.

Several people have called me over the years to ask what to do about an injured bird. I am always struck when they say something like, "It's actually in pretty good shape. Very alert. It just has a broken wing." Most people don't realize that a wing — in spite of the radius, ulna, and humerus — is not like an arm. It is more like a heart.

Birds were made for flight. Even birds that cannot fly now (ostriches, rheas, and penguins) evolved from birds that could. Physiologically, birds have poured everything into this ability. They are as light as can be. If you pick up a bird, you will find that as far as weight goes, it is like holding a bird-shaped pile of nothing. With a few exceptions, such as cormorants, whose need to dive easily and remain submerged outweighs the benefit of a pneumatic skeleton, birds have hollow bones; a light, horny bill instead of a toothed jaw; young that emerge from eggs laid outside the body; gonads that shrink outside of the breeding season; super-fast digestion to avoid carrying waste weight (if it seems like birds poop a lot, it's because they do); and of course, feathers.

The avian forelimb has become a wing. The wing is a powerful airfoil, curved so that the air crosses the top of the wing faster than it does the underside, creating lift. Flapping provides thrust. A Peregrine Falcon will pull her wings close in a dive, reducing drag; a crow playing in the wind will do the same, giving herself a thrilling swoop. Feathers on top of the wing are lifted to increase drag, slowing a bird for landing.

But how to live without a forelimb? No arm, no hand, no front paw? No other terrestrial vertebrate has managed such a life. Birds have more cervical vertebrae than mammals or reptiles, so they can stretch their necks for food and also reach around to preen hard-to-access areas. It's captivating to watch the contortions birds twist themselves into as they reach for the oil gland beneath the base of their tails, then use their bills and feet to work the protective oil into each feather. The bills of many birds, crows included, are capable of fine motor activities, and they function very much like hands—tweezing, preening, moving and carrying objects, and building nests.

. . .

I hadn't seen Charlotte for nearly a week and was beginning to be concerned. Finding her again, I smile. Charlotte might be thin and slumped, but she managed to learn to fly on one leg—no mean accomplishment. I wonder, what does it mean to have no hope when there is a radiant, earth-loving child singing in the bathroom and a broken-legged bird that has learned to fly in your tree? Still, it seems that the best prospect for a flourishing, ecologically vibrant, evolutionarily rich earth would be a massive, brutal overturning of the human population followed by several millennia of planetary recovery. Surely this doesn't count as hope. But here we are, intricate human animals capable of feeling despair over the state of the earth and, simultaneously, joy in its unfolding wildness, no matter how hampered. What are we to do with such a confounding vision? The choices appear to be few. We can deny it, ignore it, go insane with its weight, structure it into a stony ethos with which we beat our friends and ourselves to death—or we can live well in its light.

At the monastery, I keep mainly to myself, dining with the other few guests and sometimes visiting with a couple of monks who have become my friends. Some of the monks wander the grounds in black robes that brush the grass while black-feathered crows circle the surrounding agricultural land. At meals, the guest master reads to the gathered guests from the Rule of Benedict, just a snippet. When he reaches the end over the course of three months or so, he starts over. On this visit, he is back to the prologue, my favorite part. "Listen!" it rigorously begins. And how? With "the ear of the heart." Here Benedict sets himself apart from the intellectual Platonic tradition, grounding his work in the experiential—*heart* is a word that comes up often. "The question is," he writes, "will we fulfill the duties of an inhabitant?" This, I realize, is my question. Now, more than ever, I think of Benedict's unsparing exhortation in relation to the problem that has grounded my up-and-down year of learning, study, watching, and on-and-off mental shakiness: how to live. And not just as a decent human, but as an *inhabitant*—an elegant and perfect word—an inhabitant of an earthly community that has never been more troubled. Benedict's answer is beautiful: we *run* toward our "great work," and not in fear, but *joyfully*. I do not think this means we will not despair. The honesty of our despair may preclude blind hope, but it need not preclude joy or action based in love.

And besides, blind hope is not the only sort. In the monastery library, I find this definition: hope is "that virtue by which we take responsibility for the future." Not just responsibility for our individual futures but also for that of the world. Hope gives our duties a "special urgency." Hope is a *virtue*, a term that can sometimes sound primly moralistic, but the definition I find is just as expansive as the one for hope: *virtue* is the power to realize good, to do it "*joyfully* [yes, joy again] and with perseverance in spite of obstacles."

In this light, hope is our positive orientation toward the future, a future in which we simultaneously recognize difficulty, responsibility, and delight. Hope is not relative to the present situation, nor is it dependent upon a specific outcome. It has everything to do with the renewal of the earth, whatever shape that will take. Hope is not an antidote to despair, or a sidestepping of difficulty, but a companion to all of these things.

In a recent radio interview, I heard an environmental activist pitching his new book. He said part of the problem with the current climate change issues is that no one can think on a grand enough scale. Because we can't see the whole earth, we can't get a sense of the fact that our actions really do have global impact. I disagree. Obviously we can't "see the whole earth," but I do think we can develop a positive sense of our interconnection with life. Aldo Leopold spoke of "ecological perception," the confluence of knowledge and sense of connection with nature that would allow positive change. This is why the attentive inhabiting of our home place matters so immensely. As we become increasingly aware that our actions are *always* entwined with the creatures and rhythms that constitute the natural world, we begin to cultivate that outward sensibility, from our homes to the farthest-flung secret wilds and back again. This is a mystical awareness, in part, pressing the boundaries of our material skins. It comes naturally to some and is work for others. In all cases, it is a perception that can be nurtured and cultivated.

The statue of Saint Benedict in the monastery chapel is

not a good one. The colors are florid, and if it came to life, I am sure it would appear misshapen. The painted plaster crow and bread loaf portrayed next to Benedict come across much better. As the monks sing the psalms, my mind wanders. Shadowy crow shapes pass across the windows and door frame. When I hear the expression "as the crow flies," I think not just of a direct path, but also of perspective. From above, the view is a comprehensive one, a slant that sees many things at once, and their true relations. It is only a matter of several feet upward, and yet from that angle our boundaries, the terms of our relationships, the things we consider to be real and near, shift and swell. Toward earth and upward the crows fly, again and again. If I allow my perspective to be lifted by this arcing flight, these birds just might swat the poisoned bread right out of my grasping little hands.

I'm happy to return home. Home to Tom, Claire, Delilah, Charlotte, home to our pretty, imperfect household, and the round of our days, which, in the context of my own life's meaning, are no less sacred, no less wild, than those of a monastery or a forest. I look at Charlotte and consider all the human constructs she has unwittingly had heaped upon her small, common, broken body. Here is art, history, evolution, intelligence, myth, community, grace. Here is ecological disaster and ecological promise. Here is the dream of the earth: *continuance.*

I am no ecological Pollyanna. I have borne, and will continue to bear, feelings of wholehearted melancholy over the ecological state of the earth. How could I not? How could anyone not? But I am unwilling to become a hand-wringing nihilist, as some environmental "realists" seem to believe is the more mature posture. Instead, I choose to dwell, as Emily Dickinson famously suggested, in *possibility*, where we cannot predict what will happen but we make space for it, whatever it is, and realize that our participation has value. This is a grown-up optimism, where our bondedness with the rest of creation, a sense of profound interaction, and a belief in our shared ingenuity give meaning to our lives and actions on behalf of the more-than-human world.

ACKNOWLEDGMENTS

For invaluable professional guidance, I thank my literary agent nonpareil, Elizabeth Wales, and my editor at Little, Brown, Tracy Behar.

For sharing their expertise, assistance, advice, and inspiration in various guises, I am tremendously grateful to Maria Dolan, Kathryn True, Andrew Emlen, Emily Sprong, Tauna Evans, Phil Evans, Karen Kuhar, Maggie Hooks, Brian Kertson, John Marzluff, Dennis Paulson, Thomas Eisner, Kevin McGowan, Gary Luke, Idie Ulsh, Ed Newbold, David Williams, Jerry Haupt, Irene Haupt, Kelly Haupt, Ginny Furtwangler, Al Furtwangler, Ann Copeland, and Delilah.

Thank you to the folks at Whiteley Center and the University of Washington Friday Harbor Labs for providing the most beautiful place on earth to accomplish creative work (and for letting me work there!).

For their ever-ready hospitality, and for providing a quiet place to think, write, and study crows, I will always be indebted to the Benedictine sisters at St. Placid Priory, and the Benedictine monks of Mount Angel Abbey.

ACKNOWLEDGMENTS

Many thanks to the librarians at the University of Washington's Suzzallo and Allen Libraries, and the Seattle Public Libraries, and to all good librarians everywhere.

And especially, thank you with my whole heart to Tom and Claire Furtwangler.

BIBLIOGRAPHY

Barrett, John Paul. *Crows in Our Hands*. Astoria, OR: Gaff Press, 2003.

Berry, Thomas. *The Great Work: Our Way into the Future*. New York: Bell Tower, 1999.

Berry, Wendell. *Home Economics*. San Francisco: North Point Press, 1987.

Brown, Lester R. *Plan B 2.0: Rescuing a Planet Under Stress and a Civilization in Trouble*. New York: Norton, 2006.

Caffrey, C. "Correlates of Reproductive Success in Cooperatively Breeding Western American Crows: If Helpers Help, It's Not by Much." *Condor* 102 (2000): 333–41.

———. "Goal-directed Use of Objects by American Crows." *Wilson Bulletin* 113 (2001): 114–15.

———. "Tool Modification and Use by an American Crow." *Wilson Bulletin* 112 (2000): 283–84.

Carson, Rachel. *The Sense of Wonder*. New York: Harper and Row, 1956.

Chamberlain, D. R., and G. W. Cornwell. "Selected Vocalizations of the Common Crow." *Auk* 88 (1971): 613–34.

Chamberlain-Auger, J. A., P. J. Auger, and E. G. Strauss. "Breeding Biology of American Crows." *Wilson Bulletin* 102 (1990): 615–22.

Cruickshank, Helen. *Thoreau on Birds.* New York: McGraw Hill, 1964.

Deignan, Kathleen, ed. *When the Trees Say Nothing: Writings on Nature by Thomas Merton.* Notre Dame, IN: Sorin Books, 2003.

Eisner, Thomas. *For the Love of Insects.* Cambridge, MA: Belknap Press, 2003.

Elbroch, Mark. *Bird Tracks and Sign: A Guide to North American Species.* Mechanicsburg, PA: Stackpole Books, 2001.

Emery, N. J., and N. S. Clayton. "The Mentality of Crows: Convergent Evolution of Intelligence in Corvids and Apes." *Science* 306 (2004): 1903–7.

Farber, Paul. *Finding Order in Nature: The Naturalist Tradition from Linnaeus to E. O. Wilson.* Baltimore: Johns Hopkins University Press, 2000.

Feher-Elston, Catherine. *Ravensong: A Natural and Fabulous History of Ravens and Crows.* New York: Jeremy Tarcher/Penguin, 2005.

Ficken, M. S. "Avian Play." *Auk* 94 (1977): 573–82.

Franklin, R. W., ed. *The Poems of Emily Dickinson.* Cambridge, MA: Harvard University Press, 1998.

Freeman, Martha. *Always, Rachel: The Letters of Rachel Carson and Dorothy Freeman, 1952–1964.* Boston: Beacon Press, 1995.

Goodwin, Derek. *Crows of the World.* London: The British Museum, 1986.

Griffiths, Jay. *Wild: An Elemental Journey.* New York: Jeremy Tarcher/Penguin, 2006.

Haggard, Peter, and Judy Haggard. *Insects of the Pacific Northwest.* Portland: Timber Press, 2006.

Hart, Patrick, and Jonathan Montaldo, eds. *The Intimate Merton: His Life from His Journals.* San Francisco: Harper, 1999.

Heinrich, Bernd. *Mind of the Raven: Investigations and Adventures with the Wolf-Birds.* New York: HarperCollins, 1999.

Huxley, Robert, ed. *The Great Naturalists.* London: Thames and Hudson, 2007.

Hyde, Lewis, ed. *The Essays of Henry David Thoreau.* New York: North Point Press, 2002.

Kardong, Terrence. *Benedict's Rule: A Translation and Commentary.* Collegeville, MN: The Liturgical Press, 1996.

Kellert, Stephen, and E. O. Wilson, eds. *The Biophilia Hypothesis.* Washington, DC: Island Press, 1993.

Kilham, Lawrence. *The American Crow and the Common Raven.* College Station: Texas A & M University Press, 1989.

———. *On Watching Birds.* White River Jct., VT: Chelsea Green Publishing Company, 1988.

Klingle, Matthew. *Emerald City: An Environmental History of Seattle.* New Haven: Yale University Press, 2007.

Knight, R. L., D. J. Grout, and S. A. Temple. "Nest-defence behavior of the American Crow in Urban and Rural Areas." *Condor* 89 (1987): 175–77.

Lear, Linda. *Rachel Carson: Witness for Nature.* New York: Henry Holt, 1997.

Leopold, Aldo. *A Sand County Almanac.* New York: Ballantine, 1966.

Link, Russell. *Living with Wildlife in the Pacific Northwest.* Seattle: University of Washington Press, 2004.

Louv, Richard. *Last Child in the Woods: Saving Our Children from Nature-Deficit Disorder.* Chapel Hill, NC: Algonquin, 2005.

Macy, Joanna. *Coming Back to Life: Practices to Reconnect Our Lives, Our World.* Gabriola Island, British Columbia: New Society Publishers, 1998.

Madge, Steve, and Hilary Burn. *Crows and Jays.* New Jersey: Princeton University Press, 1999.

Marzluff, John, and Tony Angell. *In the Company of Crows and Ravens.* New Haven: Yale University Press, 2005.

Marzluff, John, Kevin McGowan, et al. "Causes and Consequences of Expanding American Crow Populations," in J. Marzluff, R. Bowman, and R. Donnelly, eds., *Avian Ecology and Conservation in an Urbanizing World.* Boston: Kluwer Academic Press, 2001.

McGowan, Kevin. "Demographic and Behavioral Comparisons of Suburban and Rural American Crows (*Corvusbrachyrhynchos*)," in J. Marzluff, R. Bowman, and R. Donnelly, eds., *Avian Ecology and Conservation in an Urbanizing World.* Boston: Kluwer Academic Press, 2001.

McKeon, Richard, ed. *The Basic Works of Aristotle.* New York: Random House, 1941.

Newton, Julianne Lutz. *Aldo Leopold's Odyssey: Rediscovering the Author of "A Sand County Almanac."* Washington, DC: Island Press, 2006.

Nijhuis, Michelle. "UW Professor Learns Crows Don't Forget a Face." *New York Times,* August 26, 2008.

Ödeen, Anders, and Olle Håstad. "Complex Distribution of Avian Color Vision Systems Revealed by Sequencing the SWS1 Opsin from Total DNA." *Molecular Biology and Evolution* 20 (2003): 855–61.

Oliver, Mary. *New and Selected Poems.* Boston: Beacon Press, 1992.

Partridge, Eric. *Origins: A Short Etymological Dictionary of Modern English.* New York: Greenwich House, 1983.

Pojar, Jim, and Andy MacKinnon. *Plants of the Pacific Northwest Coast.* Vancouver: Lone Pine Publishing, 1994.

Price, Jenny. *Flight Maps: Adventures with Nature in Modern America.* New York: Basic Books, 1999.

Raymo, Chet. *The Path: A One-Mile Walk Through the Universe.* New York: Walker, 2003.

Rich, Terrell D., et al. *Partners in Flight: North American Landbird Conservation Plan.* Ithaca: Cornell Lab of Ornithology, 2004.

Sax, Boria. *Crow.* London: Reaction Books, 2003.

Skutch, Alexander. *The Minds of Birds.* College Station: Texas A & M University Press, 1996.

Snyder, Gary. *The Practice of the Wild.* San Francisco: North Point, 1990.

Solnit, Rebecca. *Storming the Gates of Paradise: Landscapes for Politics.* Berkeley: University of California Press, 2007.

———. *Wanderlust: A History of Walking.* New York: Penguin, 2000.

Solomon, Andrew. *The Noonday Demon: An Atlas of Depression.* New York: Scribner, 2001.

Starke, Linda, ed. *2007 State of the World: Our Urban Future.* New York: Norton, 2007.

Strom, Deborah, ed. *Birdwatching with American Women.* New York: Norton, 1986.

Suzuki, David, ed. *When the Wild Comes Leaping Up.* Vancouver: Greystone Books, 2002.

Todd, Kim. *Tinkering with Eden: A Natural History of Exotics in America.* New York: Norton, 2002.

Turner, Jack. *The Abstract Wild.* Tucson: University of Arizona Press, 1996.

Verbeek, N. A. M., and C. Caffrey. "American Crow (Corvusbrachyrhynchos)." *The Birds of North America* 647 (A. Pool and F. Gill, eds.), 2002.

Williams, David B. *The Street-Smart Naturalist: Field Notes from Seattle.* Portland: West Winds Press, 2005.

Wilson, E. O. *Biophilia: The Human Bond with Other Species.* Cambridge, MA: Harvard University Press, 1984.

————. *Naturalist.* Washington, DC: Island Press, 1994.

Wirzba, Norman, ed. *The Art of the Commonplace: The Agrarian Essays of Wendell Berry.* Washington, DC: Counterpoint, 2002.

Withey, J. C., and J. M. Marzluff. "Dispersal by Juvenile American Crows (*Corvusbrachyrhynchos*) Influences Population Dynamics Across a Gradient of Urbanization." *Auk* 122 (2005): 206–22.

Wolch, Jennifer, and Jody Emel, eds. *Animal Geographies:*

Place, Politics, and Identity in the Nature-Culture Borderlands. New York: Verso, 1998.

Zach, R. "Shell Dropping: Decision-Making and Optimal Foraging in Northwestern Crows." *Behavior* 68 (1979): 106–17.

ABOUT THE AUTHOR

Lyanda Lynn Haupt has created and directed educational programs for Seattle Audubon, worked in raptor rehabilitation in Vermont, and been a seabird researcher for the Fish and Wildlife Service in the remote tropical Pacific. She is the author of *Pilgrim on the Great Bird Continent* and *Rare Encounters with Ordinary Birds* (winner of the 2002 Washington State Book Award). Her writing has appeared in *Image, Open Spaces, Wild Earth, Conservation Biology Journal, Birdwatcher's Digest,* and *The Prairie Naturalist.* She lives in West Seattle with her husband and daughter.